WAR IN A
DISTANT COUNTRY
AFGHANISTAN:
Invasion and Resistance

WAR IN A DISTANT COUNTRY AFGHANISTAN:
Invasion and Resistance

DAVID C. ISBY

ARMS AND
ARMOUR

Left: A group of guerrillas move out. They are lightly
equipped because they will be moving through their
own area and can stop for food or water along the route.
Movement entails, when lucky, 'ridge running' on trails
on tops, or, alternatively, the up-and-down climb over
steep contours at high altitude which leaves the
unacclimatized breathless. (David C. Isby)

First published in Great Britain in 1989 by Arms and Armour Press, Artillery House, Artillery Row, London SW1P 1RT.

Distributed in the USA by Sterling Publishing Co. Inc., 2 Park Avenue, New York, NY 10016.

Distributed in Australia by Capricorn Link (Australia) Pty. Ltd., P.O. Box 665, Lane Cove, New South Wales 2066, Australia.

British Library Cataloguing in Publication Data:

Isby, David C.
War in a distant country: Afghanistan: invasion and resistance.
1. Afghanistan. Guerrilla Wars
I. Title
958'.1044
ISBN 0-85368-769-2

The illustrations in this book have been collected from many sources, and vary in quality owing to the variety of circumstances under which they were taken and preserved. As a result, certain of the illustrations are not of the standard to be expected from the best of today's equipment, materials and techniques. They are nevertheless included for their inherent information value, to provide an authentic visual coverage of the subject.

Designed and edited by DAG Publications Ltd. Designed by David Gibbons; edited by Michael Boxall; layout by Cilla Eurich; typeset by Ronset Typesetters Ltd.; camerawork by M&E Reproductions, North Fambridge, Essex; printed and bound in Great Britain by The Bath Press, Avon.

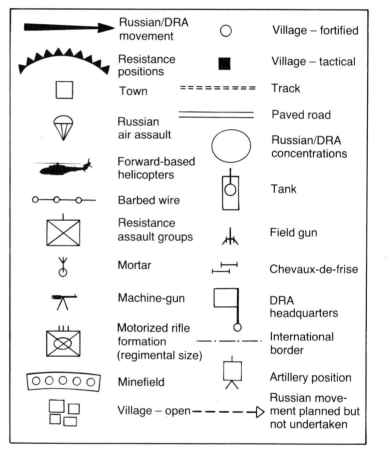

➤ Russian/DRA movement	○ Village – fortified
Resistance positions	■ Village – tactical
□ Town	========= Track
Russian air assault	——— Paved road
Forward-based helicopters	Russian/DRA concentrations
○–○–○ Barbed wire	Tank
Resistance assault groups	Field gun
Mortar	Chevaux-de-frise
Machine-gun	DRA headquarters
Motorized rifle formation (regimental size)	—·—·— International border
○○○○○ Minefield	Artillery position
Village – open	– – –▷ Russian movement planned but not undertaken

Jacket illustrations:
Front: A group of Afghan guerrillas prepare to move out of their stronghold. The stronghold (*jabha*, or front) has been the basic element of the Resistance; usually away from the main roads or towns, offensive actions were undertaken some distance away from it. In some areas, such as the Kunar or Paktia, strongholds would be established close to Kabul regime fortifications, which could then be kept under permanent siege. (US Information Agency)

Back, top: This Mi-4 Hound helicopter of the Kabul regime Air Force, shot down in Nuristan in 1979, was one of the first helicopters lost in the war. Soon afterwards, regime forces pulled out of Nuristan and have not tried to re-assert direct control since. Rather, they have tried an approach of indirect control, supporting different groups to divide the local Afghans, including supplying their factions by helicopter. If the Soviets were to withdraw from all or part of Afghanistan, they could try and apply this approach on a national scale. (US Information Agency)

Back, bottom: Captured Soviet 7.62mm PKM general-purpose machine-gun in action with the Resistance; a favourite weapon, but its 7.62mmx54 rifle ammunition is not interchangeable with the Kalashnikov and so is difficult to obtain. (*Committee for a Free Afghanistan*, Ben Pendleton)

CONTENTS

Acknowledgements: The author would like to thank The Committee for a Free Afghanistan (Washington, DC), Anthony and Ruth Arnold, Joseph Collins, John Hill, Thomas Johnson, Anne Shackleton and Andrew Smith for their valuable help, but most especially the many people involved in the Afghanistan issue who have shared their knowledge, and the Afghans themselves, without whom there would be no book and who have given much not only to their conflict, but to the world itself.

INTRODUCTION

'How horrible, fantastic, incredible it is that we should be digging trenches and trying on gas masks because of a quarrel in a far-away country between people of whom we know nothing.' The speaker was Neville Chamberlain. The faraway country was Czechoslovakia at the height of the crisis of 1938 which led to the Munich meeting and its subsequent agreement. The sentiment is familiar, for bombs are always incredible until they fall. In the mid-1970s, Afghans would have considered the idea of a war with the Soviet Union even more incredible. Afghanistan was the Soviet Union's best neighbour. Afghan foreign policy was neutral, it was part of no alliance that could be construed as anti-Soviet, and had firm diplomatic and economic links across the northern border. The war was unthinkable until it started.

For Chamberlain to have called Czechoslovakia a faraway country was parochial in his age of wireless and 200mph aircraft. But, today, Afghanistan is a distant country, even in an age of instant communications. It is distant not only in miles but also in culture. It is distant too because the bombs, real in Afghanistan, are still incredible in the West.

What will emerge from the War in Afghanistan? The Soviets may well have learned that their army has not been the best tool for consolidating power in Afghanistan. It may be, in the future, that the Soviet Union will apply political or military pressure against Iran or Pakistan, either as part of a 'grand design' or exploiting, opportunistically, instability. Whether the Soviet withdrawal proves to be total or not, the outcome of the war may not even be determined by what government, at the end of the day, sits in Kabul, but rather how Southern Asia, and the world, has changed.

This book is an outgrowth of my visits to the Afghan Resistance in 1984, 1985, 1987 and 1988, updated to November 1988. It is not a memoir and still less an adventure. It is a briefing on Afghanistan, of the sort I am often asked to give at staff colleges, conferences, and similar jolly gatherings, and it emphasizes the military aspect of the war.

Chamberlain claimed to know nothing of the people of Czechoslovakia. In 1988 to claim the same about Afghanistan would require wilful ignorance. While Afghanistan has hardly been headline news at any time since 1978, there has been a great deal of reporting, some of it quite good. This book aims to provide some of the context for the story of Afghanistan as it emerges in the news and becomes history.

Below: A Soviet T-62 moves down a road near Kandahar – into a Resistance ambush which was sprung seconds after this photograph was taken. The flat terrain near Kandahar makes ambushes relatively deadly, while in more mountainous areas they tend to be launched at longer range, from high ground. The Soviets left trees growing along some of the roads around Kandahar as late as 1986. (National Islamic Front of Afghanistan)

1. A SHORT WALK WITH THE AFGHAN RESISTANCE

The Mi-17 Hip-H of the Kabul regime's air force announced its arrival by the whine of its twin Isotov turboshaft engines and the wop-wop-wop of its rotors, blowing up little clouds of dust along the side of the road it was following. It was moving fast and very low for, in 1987, the helicopter was no longer master of the skies of Afghanistan, and the Hip crews feared the new American-made Stinger surface-to-air missiles. To the Hip crew, two pilots and the two gunners behind the flexible-mounted PKM 7.62mm machine-guns with safeties off, in the fuselage doors, Afghanistan slips past in a blur. Sometimes, guerrillas will work up to the roadside under cover of darkness and wait for morning to shoot the road-running Hips with RPG-7 anti-tank rocket launchers and then run very fast and very far before the Hip crew's friends show up; but this is not going to happen today.

The guerrilla's eye view of Afghanistan is also limited, but in a different way from that of the Hip crew. Sweeping geopolitical overviews tend to lose their meaning when dealing with the realities of Afghanistan which tend to be as hard in their way as the mountains are in theirs.

In a bombed-out house overlooking a valley, the war is distant. The guerrillas know by sound the weapons they hear; the difference between the 'beast-o-yek' multiple rocket launchers—the 122mm BM-21 and the bigger 'mushak', the 220mm BM-27. Sometimes, if the projectiles burst nearby, there will be a thud, a fountaining of earth upwards, and rolling clouds of yellow dust from the impact. Sometimes, the ruins of buildings will disappear in sudden eruptions of stone dust from the rockets.

The Soviets never lacked firepower to kill all the Resistance, the problem was knowing where to apply it. Making the rubble bounce

is not the answer, so more often the targets have been the civilian population. The war turned the Afghans into the world's largest refugee population: more than three million in Pakistan, one million in Iran, two million internally, and 100,000 elsewhere. That is why there are no more civilians in the burst pattern of that particular rocket battery. In the border area of the Kunar Valley, most of the guerrilla's families are either dead or in refugee camps, but starting in 1987 a few farmers returned to tend their fields which they had abandoned in the face of years of intensive bombing. They had discovered that the crews of the fighter-bombers were almost as wary of the Stinger as those of the road-running Hip.

Resistance response to the multiple rocket-launcher, in its turn, comes from a single 82mm mortar, aimed at a position that may contain an artillery observer together with the usual garrison of teenage boys in the uniform of the Kabul Regime's army. The Chinese mortar is new, its olive-green paint still glossy, its metalwork shiny and slightly oily, like the bicycles on sale in Peshawar bazaar: well-made, old technology. Some Afghans jerk mortars around by their tripod and aim by pointing them in the general direction of the enemy. One Afghan understands the principles of indirect fire, or at least makes a good show, fussing with the sight and the elevation screw. He has a landmark which serves as an aiming stake, for the mortar stays put in the one stronghold—witnessed by the discarded ammunition containers—and does not engage many targets. The mortar shells are extracted from olive-drab wooden boxes, that will later serve as building material or cooking fuel, and enthusiastically dressed and fuzed. Leaving the tube, they sound like a refrigerator door being slammed hard and explode, seconds later, at about their maximum 3-kilometre range, making more modest puffs of smoke than the Soviet rockets. There is no sign of their effect. But the Afghans feel it has been a good shoot.

Throughout the war the guerrillas have seen the Soviets mainly in helicopters or aircraft. If they are going about their business, they appear only as contrails, high in the blue sky. If they are looking for you, the first pass by a MiG or a helicopter popping up from behind a ridge may be the only warning. The Soviet, or Kabul regime troops, run convoys through the valleys escorted by tanks and the six-wheeled BTR-60PB APCs which look like little beetles from the high ground. Regularly, the Afghans leave their strongholds to ambush these 'beetles' and the line of trucks following them.

But the bodies and the destruction left by the men in the APCs are real. The trail of mangled corpses and smoking villages which the Soviets have left across Afghanistan is no atrocity propaganda. No guerrilla war is pleasant, nor is any war fought against Soviets, be they Tsarist or Communist, who are always brave and stubborn in battle and never given to gentleness, forgiveness, or mistaking war for sport.

To the Afghan guerrilla, the war has been a series of helicopters either evaded or fired upon, of people encountered, of long walks and little food, and, if he is unlucky, of destruction and desolation. What he knows of the overall picture comes largely from the radio; BBC, Voice of America, and Radio Tehran are listened to with intense interest. In 1987 and 1988, these sources started to carry more and more news of a Soviet withdrawal, of a new government in Kabul, and maybe even, the ever hoped for event: an end to the war. This was discussed over many cups of *chin chai*, heavy with dissolved sugar, and the guerrillas remain sceptical long after the bureaucrats in Washington and elsewhere had come to the conclusion that it was endgame in Afghanistan.

It has been a long war, and many people in the Western world have probably read articles about the brave men who, starting with little else but a few hand-held weapons, have fought the world's most powerful armed forces every day of every year since

Christmas, 1979. Throughout that time, they have really meant it when they say that they are not going to stop fighting until they are all dead or exhausted, and they remain a brave and resolute people.

For Brezhnev and the Politburo to think they would easily beat people like this was a very big mistake. The man with the henna-red beard who could carry an astonishing number of other people's kit; the woman—unseen except for a brief flash of bright clothing by the door—who cooked one of her last chickens for a foreign guest; the *maulavi* who patiently explained, through an interpreter, that God made man, unlike a sheep, not to submit but to fight: these are Afghanistan. They have not been defeated, and why they have not been defeated has an importance reaching beyond their still-distant country.

Above: A *mujahed*, his beard coloured with red henna, a custom in parts of Pashto-speaking Afghanistan. (David C. Isby)

Top right: An Afghan 82mm M-1937 mortar. This weapon, limited by its 3-kilometre range, has seen much combat. Discarded shell containers can indicate an often-used firing position.

Right: The author having tea with some Afghan friends. (David C. Isby)

2. BACKGROUND TO WAR

Afghans and Afghanistan

Who are the people who have fought the Soviet Army? Of a pre-war population estimated in the 14–18 million range (probably about 15.5 million), the major ethnic group was the Pushtu-speaking Pathans of the east and south (about 42 per cent of the population). Afghanistan's leaders were traditionally Pathan, and the term 'Afghan' was itself originally seen as synonymous with Pathan. Divided into tribes and clans, predominantly Sunni with some Shia, they set the course of much of Afghan culture. Most of the refugees currently in Pakistan are Pathan, which has altered the ethnic picture. The Dari-speaking Tadjiks of the north and west were about 23 per cent of the population. They lack the Pathan's tribal divisions. While the Pathans feel kinship with brother Pathans in the North-West Frontier Province of Pakistan (which has led to the Afghan government's irredentist claims on all the land to the banks of the Indus), the Tadjiks' fellows were in the Soviet Union's Tadjikistan Socialist Republic.

The Turkomen and Uzbeks of the north each speak their own Turkic language. Many of these people were originally from what is now the Soviet Union, and their families were driven out by the Soviet war against them in the 1920s and 1930s. A few Turkic-speaking Kirghiz, living among the Pamirs, were driven out from Afghanistan by 1980.

The Mongol-descended Hazaras are distinctive in their appearance, and by being Shia Muslims. They are concentrated in the Hazara Jat, mountainous, isolated and poor even by Afghan standards. Even more isolated and yet poorer are the Nuristanis. Fewer in number than the Hazaras, they are an ancient people of Mediterranean origin who practised their own religion (with, as Kipling wrote, 'two and thirty idols') until forcibly converted to Sunni Islam towards the end of the last century. Nuristan is in the fastness of the eastern Hindu Kush. Baluchis, relatively few in number, live in the arid south and competed with Pathans for access to the scantily watered land, and looked across the border to kinsmen in Pakistan and Iraq. Kuchi and Aimaq nomads, their migrations now limited by the war, once ranged throughout much of the country. In west Afghanistan, there are also ethnic Shia Persians, known as Farsiwan.

Being at the crossroads of Asia and the diversity of race and culture may have contributed to the degree of toleration that has traditionally existed in Afghanistan. The intra-communal violence endemic to the sub-continent never took root. But if Afghanistan was not Lebanon, with religiously divided communities making up a powder-keg that finally detonated in 1975, neither was it a peaceful and prosperous Switzerland.

From 1747 to 1978, the Pathans had what centralized power there was in Afghanistan, wielded by the monarchy and its successors and their supporters, all generally Pathan 'notables'. This was not necessarily popular with the other ethnic groups in Afghanistan nor, indeed, with all the Pathans, and led to a tradition of armed resistance against centralized authority. To suppress this resistance has been the main reason for the existence of the Afghan armed forces.

The mountains of Afghanistan are not teeming with pacifists. Each individual Afghan group (*qawm* in Dari), defined in

Left: 'Ridge running', moving on the tops of ridges, behind the crest, is relatively easy. The hard part is getting to the next ridge. (David C. Isby)

either religious, geographic, tribal, or kinship terms, considers itself autonomous and greatly dislikes outside interference. Afghan society, especially that of the Pathans, has a tradition of resistance to outside authority and its imposition, whether the scope is international (the resistance to the British in the three Afghan wars); national (the tradition of local rebellion, limited but armed, against Kabul-based authority in pre-1978 Afghanistan); or local authority (the sway of village, tribe, clan, or *khan* not one's own). Afghan society has a large traditional element of conflict. Afghan nationalism, previously weak in a country where local sentiment was strong and Kabul largely irrelevant, has been forged in the course of the war, where there is a greater sense of fighting a national war. Those fighting now realize that they have much more in common with their fellow Afghans than they might previously have thought.

This has led to a society that was framed for resistance, but one that it is very hard for anyone to organize. The warrior-poet remains, as he has for centuries, the Afghan ideal. The background of Afghan society has produced fighting men who are committed, tough, implacable and tremendously brave. Traditional Pathan society, like that of other mountain peoples such as Scots highlanders and American hillbillies, experienced inter-tribal and inter-group feuding. This warfare, which could be over agricultural rights, land, or dominance, could be remarkably long-running. Much of the reason lies in *Pushtuwali*, the traditional code of the Pathan. Among its requirements is *badal*: revenge. A Pathan must avenge a blow, either from the one who gave it or from one of his kith and kin, even if it takes many generations. This

has led to blood feuds being passed from father to son. But this fighting, while endemic, was also limited. The aim was to right perceived wrongs, not to dispossess or enslave opponents. The brightly coloured dresses traditionally worn by Pathan women were supposedly to protect them from snipers. *Pushtuwali* has its requirements for peaceful life, but none for submission. It is, in the words of the anthropologist, Dr Louis Dupree, 'a stringent code, a tough code for tough men, who of necessity live tough lives'.

Afghanistan is unified by religion—a uniquely Afghan form of Islam. The same tradition of the independent *qawm* also applies to religious authority, and Afghans are suspicious of outside religious leaders; even orthodox Sunni Islam, in Afghanistan, is heavily influenced by local forms of Sufism. The Shia concept of the *imam* as sole link between man and religion is particularly alien to most Afghans. Predominantly Sunni, with some Ismailis among a 15–20 per cent Shia minority, Afghanistan has never had a strong, central religious leader but this has never limited the strength of the religion and the fierce piety of the people.

Ever since Afghanistan was established as a nation in 1747 by the first Pathan King, Ahmad Durrani Shah, it has been politically de-centralized due to its predominantly mountainous or desert terrain; poor communications (no railways and a limited network of paved roads); ethnic, linguistic and religious divisions; and the wishes of its people. Traditionally, Kabul did not try to meddle in local affairs. Before the war, the authority of the central government was limited and most Afghan decision-making was by local meeting (*jirga*), and the local

THE AFGHANS

In his classic 1815 work, *An Account of the Kingdom of Caubul*, Mountstuart Elphinstone seems to have held a view of the Afghan character that has remained clear and convincing to this day:

'To sum up the character of the Afghans in a few words; their vices are revenge, envy, avarice, rapacity, and obstinacy; on the other hand, they are fond of liberty, faithful to their friends, kind to their dependents, hospitable, brave, hardy, frugal, laborious, and prudent; and they are less disposed than the nations in their neighbourhood to falsehood, intrigue, and deceit.'

Above: Guerrillas at prayer. The importance of Islam to the Resistance cannot be over-estimated. One reason a post-war Afghanistan is unlikely to become another Lebanon is because of the unifying impact of Islam, especially the Sunni Islam shared by 80 per cent of the population. (Massoud Khalili, *Jamiat-e-Islami* Afghanistan)

khan, *malik*, or *mullah* (headman, chief, or religious man) remained strong outside the cities. Unity has been rare, imposed either by foreigners or by strong leaders such as Ahmad Durrani Shah and Abdur Rahman Khan, who pulled the tribes and villages together after the Second Afghan War.

Summers are hot and dry, the winters cold, especially in the higher country, and from November to mid-March snow makes travel difficult. Campaigning on the ground is often reduced in the winter. The Hindu Kush runs like a spine, east to west, ending in the tall, snow-capped Pamir Mountains in the Wakhan Corridor; created to prevent a Russo-Indian border in the nineteenth century, it is now reputed to have been possibly annexed by the Soviet Union through a secret treaty.

The Hindu Kush follows, roughly, the linguistic dividing line, with the Pathans to the south. North of the Hindu Kush are more mountains, fading northwards into the arid steppes of Central Asia. The flat areas of northern Afghanistan are around Mazar-e-Sharif, with its great blue mosque, and between the Soviet Union and Herat. In the west, the Iranian plateau runs to Herat (on the old silk route to Central Asia and China) and Shindand, with its airbase, then rises into the Hindu Kush. The central Hazara Jat is in the midst of the high mountains. The south and south-east are largely desolate, rocky deserts, with agriculture limited to irrigated areas.

Agriculture was the primary occupation of the Afghan people, but only 15 per cent of the land was cultivated, and this was concentrated in the river valleys or other irrigated areas. Even in the days of peace, Afghanistan was one of the world's twenty poorest nations (imagine whom you have to beat to be in that league). It does, however, possess substantial reserves of natural gas and other resources that have never been fully exploited. The Soviets, however, have pumped the natural gas for their own use (offsetting the cost against the war effort) throughout their war in Afghanistan. But no one would want to occupy Afganistan for its natural resources although future develop-ment may change this.

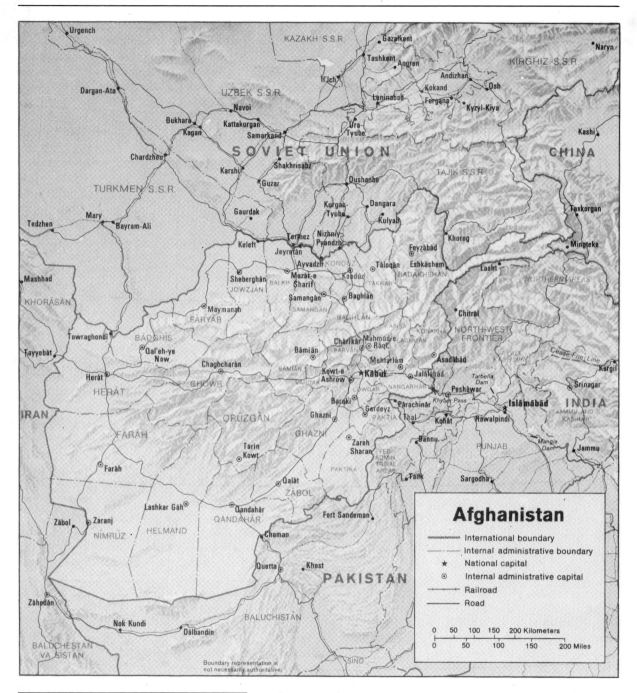

The Great Game to 1973

Like the Soviet Union, imperial Russia, did not regard a border as secure until it had troops on both sides of it. For Afghanistan, this first started to matter in the 1820s and 1830s. The Soviet Empire embarked upon a campaign of eastern colonial expansion, acquiring a vast range of subject peoples, in line with the behaviour of other colonial powers at the time, but while the other empires have since faded away Central Asia remains subject to Moscow.

Long before the Soviet advance reached the borders of Afghanistan, it had become a matter of concern to the British in India.

This was the start of 'the great game' of pre-1914 power politics in Central and Southern Asia. The British viewed Afghanistan as a buffer state against Soviet and Persian expansionism, needed to secure the frontiers of India against incursion and insurrection. This led to the British involvement in Afghanistan, using internal Afghan unrest to establish a military presence in the First Afghan War (1839–42). Although a British military victory, the complete annihilation of the British forces originally garrisoned in Kabul made a lasting impression on the British. In 1878, after a generation of peace with Afghanistan. the British again went to war with the Afghans, largely to ensure that the government in Kabul did not become pro-Soviet. The Second Afghan War (1878–81), despite costly battlefield setbacks, was also a British military victory. In the wake of the war, the British retained control of Afghan foreign affairs and they put Abdur Rahman Khan on the throne. Far from being a puppet, he made his life's work the centralizing of Afghanistan, turning it into a modern nation. His last words, to his heirs, were, 'Never trust the Soviets.'

The Tsar's armies, however, had extended their sway to Afghanistan's northern borders. In 1885, the Soviets seized the Afghan territory of Panjdeh. Fear that they would march on Herat and Kabul led to threats of war from London and negotiations resulted in Russia's recognizing Afghanistan's northern borders in 1887.

With the strong Abdur Rahman in power until 1901 and British power at its zenith, Afghanistan's borders only became turbulent again with the Bolshevik Revolution. In Soviet-controlled Central Asia, nationalist leaders emerged. Some made common cause with the Reds, but most were sworn to regain full independence. In 1919, Afghanistan provoked the Third Afghan War against a Great Britain weakened by the world war and harassed by the unrest in India. While this short war was, again, militarily a British victory, it led to the removal of British control of Afghan foreign policy.

Diplomatic exchanges between Afghanistan and the Soviet Union began as the cannon cooled in 1919. Even with the Civil War still going on, in September 1920, the Soviets pledged aid to Afghanistan and delivered 5,000 Moisin-Nagant rifles to help repel imperialism. The 1921 Treaty of Friendship codified Soviet-Afghan relations.

Although the Red Army was waging war in Central Asia against the Muslim population, Afghanistan used its new foreign policy independence to become the first neighbouring country to recognize Lenin's regime. A further treaty was signed in 1926, but the continuing war in Central Asia strained Soviet-Afghan relations. At times, the Royal Afghan Government supported the resistance, but this was limited by the internal divisions of Afghan politics, which remained extremely unstable throughout the period. This led to Soviet involvement in Afghan politics, and incursions across the border, and the Afghan Government halted its cross-border aid to the resistance inside the Soviet Union by 1931. Treaties in 1931 and 1936 re-affirmed the Soviet position. Meanwhile, Afghanistan's own internal unrest peaked in 1928–33, ending when Mohammed Zahir Shah began his reign as king.

The British left the borders of Afghanistan in 1947. In their wake the Afghan Government decided to press irredentist claims to Pakistan's North-West Frontier Province which led to strained relations between the two Islamic nations (and Pakistan's ally, the United States throughout the 1950s and 1960s. From 1953 to 1963, under prime minister Prince Mohammed Daoud Khan, Afghanistan looked to the Soviet Union for aid and trade and, traditionally opposed to foreign alliances, would not enter into the US-supported Baghdad Pact. By the 1950s Afghanistan was considered to be in the Soviet sphere of influence. Aid was the Soviet Union's most effective foreign policy tool in Afghanistan: Afghan troops were trained and re-equipped along Soviet lines by large numbers of military advisors; the Soviets built irrigation systems, dams, roads (generously stressing the bridges for 50-ton loads) and airfields. American and other foreign donors contributed a number of key projects, but did not match the scope of Soviet aid.

Afghanistan's move from an absolute to a constitutional monarchy started in the 1950s. The 1964 constitution completed this

process, and parliamentary elections were held in 1965. During this change, two rival underground Communist parties, the *Khalq* ('masses') and the *Parcham* ('banner') were formed (to be united only on paper in 1965 as the People's Democratic Party of Afghanistan) [PDPA]. Formed by a handful of intellectuals, ideologues, and Soviet agents, all disenchanted by the backwardness of Afghanistan, they did not do well in elections, securing only four of 216 seats in the 1965 Parliament and two in the 1969 Parliament. So they started to concentrate more on underground organization, their ideology diverging until *Khalq* believed in the necessity of destructive violence, to be aimed at Afghan society, while the *Parcham* became servilely pro-Soviet.

The other critics of the situation in Afghanistan were Islamist. Also disenchanted by the King's rule and the slowness of development, they looked to Islamic principles and values, beyond traditional Afghan religious ways.

All of this was taking place in Kabul, the only real city in Afghanistan, with its university, airport, and, above all, its intellectual life. Kabul was a thriving city. Women were becoming doctors and lawyers, and many stopped wearing the *shadri* (veil). Short-wave radios, improved agriculture and other innovations were bringing progress even to the rural areas. In the early 1970s, the countryside itself was relatively peaceful and developing, although major crop failures necessitated widespread aid efforts to avert famine. Most of the ferment in pre-war Afghanistan was limited to the educated class in which everyone knew everyone else. This was to add much to the bitterness of the years that were to come.

Slouching Towards Disaster: 1973–8

Daoud, forced from power by the King during the constitutional monarchy period, made common cause with others discontented with Afghan government—the Communists. While the PDPA was still a

Above: The Duralamin Palace, scene of the heaviest fighting on 27 December 1979, was Zahir Shah's residence from the 1930s to 1973. It was taken over by Soviet military advisors to the Kabul regime – hence the antennae – for much of the war.

small party (only 2,000–6,500 strong even in the early 1980s), the *Khalq* had a following among teachers, journalists, field and junior grade military officers and among some de-tribalized rural Pathans; the *Parcham* were largely white-collar, Dari-speaking and Kabul-based. *Khalq* had the weight of numbers.

While the King was out of the country, Daoud struck. The *coup* of 17 July 1973, made him President and ended the Afghan monarchy, the King going into exile in Rome where (in 1988) he remains. Daoud re-warded his Communist allies with some cabinet posts. His policy stressed closer relations with the Soviet Union and this, in turn, led to greater tension with Pakistan.

Within a year, however, Daoud realized that the PDPA's interests were closer to those of Moscow than to his own and to consolidate his own power he eventually removed five *Parcham* PDPA Ministers who had formed part of the original government (the hardline *Khalqis* had been excluded). He re-asserted the traditional Afghan balance-of-power neutrality by accepting an exten-sive aid package from Iran (the Shah wanted a stable neighbour) in 1976. Daoud also took steps to lessen the Soviet influence that had greatly increased in the first years of his government by reducing the number of Soviet advisers.

One of the reasons Daoud shifted course was because of Islamic opposition, rising in Afghanistan throughout the 1970s, nurtured at Kabul University and abroad. It chal-lenged first the King's, and then Daoud's rule, as being corrupt. To the Islamists, government should be formed in accordance with the word of God and the desire of the people. Many Islamist leaders had gone into exile and were calling for armed resistance to what they saw as a pro-Soviet govern-ment.

Soon, Daoud was trying to mend relations with Pakistan; he had tried to support Baluchi insurgents there and Pakistan had returned the favour by funding Islamist opponents of Daoud's regime, including Gulbuddin Hekmatyar, a former activist at Kabul University, and training anti-Daoud insurgents, one of whom, an engineering student named Ahmad Shah Massoud, went home to the Panjshir Valley, north of Kabul,

to try (unsuccessfully) to lead a revolt in 1975.

In 1977 Daoud called a *Loya Jirga*, the estates of Afghanistan, relying on traditional Afghan ways rather than relying on the PDPA or the Islamists. In a new constitution, introduced in 1977, he named personal supporters to key positions and only his own National Revolutionary Party was permitted to operate legally.

The Soviets realized that Daoud was unlikely to be able to remove Afghanistan from their sphere of influence. What was changing, however, was the Soviets' view of developing nations, and their willingness to become more directly involved. In the 1970s, they saw the global correlation of forces altering, and they became more active not just in Afghanistan, but in conflicts throughout the Third World, convinced that in the wake of Vietnam and Watergate, American power, prestige, and will were in irreversible retreat. This spirit of Brezhnev-era globalism was seen most strongly in Afghanistan.

While an uneasy peace reigned during the mid-1970s, other wheels were already turning. The PDPA (*Khalq* and *Parcham* reunited in July 1977), in close co-operation with their Soviet friends, were back underground, plotting. However, one of the drawbacks of this would-be Leninist vanguard party now became apparent: many of its members were good companions and co-conspirators, but most were astonish-ingly stupid politically, and frequently inept. But fortune, too often, favours not the brave, but the brutal.

1978–9

In 1978, following the murder of a Com-munist theoretician—probably the result of PDPA feuding but blamed on Daoud—the outpouring of anti-regime sentiment in Kabul panicked Daoud. He had key PDPA members rounded up, but hesitated and failed to move against the Communists in the military. It is uncertain how much was planned and how much was improvisation; but if the Soviets did not order the resulting *putsch* by Army units led by *Khalq* officers, they certainly knew it was coming. On 24 April 1978, Daoud was overthrown and, with his entire family, executed. While the 1973 *coup* had been relatively bloodless, casualties this time numbered over 1–2,000 dead. The PDPA was now in control of the Democratic Republic of Afghanistan (DRA).

After a month of shared rule, the *Khalq* party took over in a post-*coup* power struggle, due in part to its army links. It not only purged the remains of Daoud's and the king's government, but their fellow Communists in the *Parcham* party—previously supported by the Soviets—as well. Nur Mohammed Taraki, the *Khalq* president and prime minister, now received the full support of the Soviet Union. A Treaty of Friendship and Good Neighbourliness was signed in December and more Soviet mili-

tary equipment, advisers for the DRA armed forces and government, and development aid was provided.

In a policy composed in equal parts of brutality, stupidity and ineptitude, the *Khalq* regime set about turning Afghanistan into a Brummagem Stalinist Russia. Every facet of Islamic and Afghan life was to be forced into line with their simplistic understanding of Marxism-Leninism—the *Khalqis* were not ones for fine distinctions or theorizing.

The split within the PDPA parties, while deep, paled before the broader division between the PDPA and the population as a whole. The PDPA visualized its role as a 'Leninist vanguard', hauling a reluctant people into socialism, but the gap between party and people was certainly greater than in any comparable nation where Communist

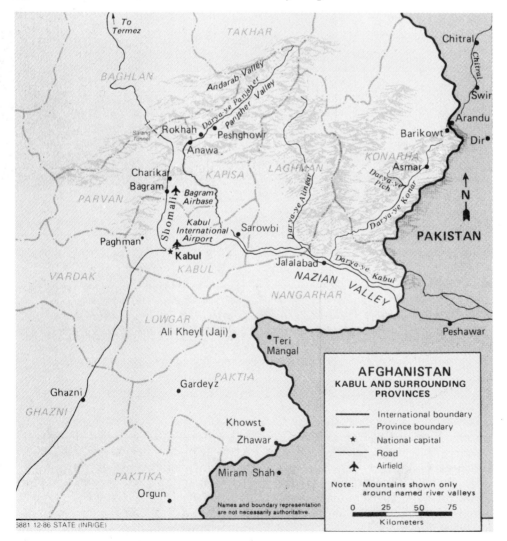

AFGHANISTAN
KABUL AND SURROUNDING PROVINCES

—————— International boundary
—·—·—·— Province boundary
★ National capital
—————— Road
✈ Airfield

Note: Mountains shown only around named river valleys

0   25   50   75
Kilometers

Names and boundary representation are not necessarily authoritative.

5881 12-86 STATE (INR/GE)

Above: The Kunar Valley, scene of much fighting throughout the war. The road along the river has Communist outposts along its length at this point, and so by 1987 helicopters would road-run along it. The Communist fortifications in this photo were eventually evacuated in May 1988.

power had been successfully consolidated.

In 1978, the vast majority of Afghans saw the *Khalq* programme as anti-Islamic actions by a regime that now also appeared to be a tool of foreign 'infidels'; land was seized and given to collectives or smaller farmers; symbols such as the replacement of the Islamic green in the national flag by Soviet red aroused widespread opposition; farm credit was nationalized, paralyzing much agriculture; Afghan ways in education and family life were attacked at village level by Party activists sent from Kabul, who increasingly fell victim to violently expressed peasant outrage. The Army, its *Khalq* officers still only a minority, started to show a reluctance to look for the people who had squeezed the trigger on these brash young men from Kabul who held such contempt for the people in the villages. The Kabul regime's policy of hostility to Islam was the catalyst in creating a nationwide

(albeit disjointed) resistance that had never before been seen in Afghanistan or, indeed, in Southern or Central Asia.

Unrest was apparent in Kabul too, leading to demonstrations and violence. In February 1979 the American Ambassador was kidnapped by what were said to be Maoist anti-government forces. He was then killed in a botched rescue attempt by Soviet-advised Kabul regime Sarandoy security forces, trained by East Germans who had replaced the West Germans associated with the now-disbanded Gendarmerie.

The Kabul regime began to find itself at war with its own people. By the summer of 1978, Nuristan, Badakhshan, and much of the Kunar Valley was in open revolt. Anti-PDPA sentiment linked traditionalists (the supporters of old, village Afghanistan) and the Islamist opposition. By early 1979, there was armed resistance in 25 of Afghanistan's 28 provinces. The resistance fighters called

Left: Kabul, December, 1979: check-points of Soviet paratroopers on all major roads. This was the sight that greeted many residents of the city on 27 December. Many never approached the check-point; they just turned back and headed out of town, for the hills and the Resistance. (US Information Agency)

Left: Since the Herat rising of 21 March 1979, the Hind attack helicopter has been the symbol of the Soviet war in Afghanistan. Helicopter tactics are one area where the Soviet lessons of Afghanistan are directly applicable to tactics as a whole. (US Information Agency)

themselves *mujahideen* (fighters for the faith) and their struggle a *jihad* (war for the faith). Kabul regime units, previously reluctant to fight, started to desert with their weapons.

This happened in Herat on 21 March 1979 when anti-Communist demonstrators seized control of the city. Many of the Kabul regime troops sent to disperse them, led by a Major Ismael Khan, instead joined the crowd in a hunt for the people they held responsible for the war— the Soviets. Dozens were put to death in traditional Afghan ways. The Kabul regime counter-attacked with fresh and loyal troops; shootings and airstrikes, including the first flown by Soviet aircrews, left up to 5,000 dead. Taraki's legitimacy was shaken, and Deputy Prime Minister Hafizullah Amin now assumed the mantle of strong man of the Kabul regime, becoming Prime Minister on 27 March.

Attempting to restore the situation, Amin took his new Soviet hardware—especially Mi-24 Hind helicopters—and advisers into the field for military offensives throughout Afghanistan. In April, a drive up the Kunar Valley encountered bitter resistance, leading to a number of large-scale massacres of civilians. In the town of Kerala, more than a thousand were machine-gunned, and refugees started to pour over the border to Pakistan.

Other offensives went poorly, despite more Soviet advisers and helicopters. A tribal *lashkar* was raised in Wardak for the Kabul regime by an ex-Royal Army colonel. While the recruitment drive was intended to be used to restore Communist rule in the Hazara Jat—an example of the use of inter-group divisions to assure centralized power as had been seen in Afghanistan since the last century—instead its leaders turned it against the Communists. A Kabul regime mechanized column was ambushed and wiped out in Paktia province in July.

To Moscow, the situation in the Soviet Union's newest satellite started to look increasingly grim, evidenced by Politburo meetings and a series of high-level visitors. With the security of the Soviet-manned helicopter force—now in daily combat—in danger, a battalion of Army paratroopers was flown into Bagram airbase near Kabul in July.

Throughout Afghanistan, Taraki's repression continued; more than 17,000 Afghans were executed, many in Kabul's Pul-e-Charki prison. (Radio Kabul admitted simply 'tens of thousands'). The non-Communist intelligentsia was systematically massacred or fled into exile. The religious leadership also were singled out as targets. The *Parcham* leadership was eliminated or were expelled from the Party. The terror led to several mutinies in army units—including the Kabul garrison—throughout 1978–9.

The Soviets feared that the events in Herat would be repeated on a larger scale since the Kabul regime army appeared weaker than ever; they realized that helicopters and advisers alone were not enough. More high-level visits revealed a deteriorating situation throughout the spring and summer of 1979, that of Deputy Minister of Defence, General A. A. Yepishev apparently being particularly telling. Meanwhile, Kabul regime military units were defeated in the Panjshir Valley and Paktia province. In Moscow, more Politburo meetings, with the ailing General Secretary Brezhnev presiding saw the consensus move towards military intervention. By October, reservists were being recalled in the border areas, routine training had stopped, and at Fergana, Kirovabad, and Vitebsk, paratroopers worked on their armoured vehicles.

Unaware of the activity in the vehicle parks north of the border, in Kabul the internal *Khalq* power struggle, raging since 1978, now escalated. Taraki and Amin ended up in a gunfight on 14 September and when Taraki died on 9 October of the usual 'natural causes'— everyone died of natural causes in Kabul in 1978–9—Amin's seizure of power was complete; the Soviets had engineered the fall of Taraki.

In the autumn of 1979, Amin tried a combination of political concessions to the Resistance, who proved uninterested, and military offensives, but it was obvious he could not control Afghanistan, or even Kabul. He also realized that the Soviets were not there to support the PDPA, but to secure their own interests.

The Soviets believed that Amin's government would not endure more than a few months. They supported PDPA acts against him. By early December, Soviet

Above: The Panjshir Valley. This shows the lower valley early in the war, before it was devastated. While obviously narrow, it remains that a Soviet division-sized force only slowly ebbed its way up it in 1984. (Committee for a Free Afghanistan)

Left: This BTR-152 of the Kabul regime army was part of a force defeated in Paktia on 17 May 1979, when a brigade of the 7th Division, led by its commanding officer, ended up deserting, many joining the Resistance. This defeat was one that convinced the Soviets of the necessity of intervention. (Committee for a Free Afghanistan)

Above right: December 1979: Soviet paratroopers on top of their BMD airborne infantry combat vehicle in Kabul. Most of the airborne forces have spent the war around Kabul literally as a 'palace guard', as contingency against a large-scale rising, on the model of Herat in 1979, to protest at the Soviet presence. (US Department of Defense)

divisions were in position to move across the Afghan border. The US Government was aware of this, but President Jimmy Carter, wanting to avoid confrontation, decided only to warn the Soviet Union against the consequences of invasion, not to go public with the information until the last days.

Meanwhile, the Soviets were making contact with the *Parcham* party members who had survived the *Khalq* purges. Elements of the 105th Guards Airborne Division had started to fly into Kabul airport in mid-December, joining Soviet Air Force units already there. On 24 December the airlift increased. Droning through the snow flurries came the Aeroflot and Air Force Antonovs and Ilyushins, one every few minutes, each carrying fit young para-troopers and their little air-droppable BMD infantry combat vehicles, armed with 73mm guns. The Salang Pass was held by a force of Soviet paratroopers, moving up the highway from Bagram.

Neither in Kabul nor in Washington was there a move, at the last minute, to prevent the conclusion of the process Moscow had started in the summer. Soviet advisers to the

DRA Army removed tank batteries 'for winterization' and called in ammunition 'for safety inspection'. Some Kabul regime officers were locked up or poisoned. Others dithered, waited for orders or were in Soviet pay (years of sending Afghan officers to the Soviet Union for professional military education had led to widespread infiltration).

On 27 December, the blow fell. Two motorized rifle divisions moved across the border, one on each of the two main routes, the 357th Motorized Rifle Division advancing Kushka–Herat–Shindand and the 360th 'Nevel-Polovsk' Motorized Rifle Division advancing Termez–Kabul–Kandahar, through the long and vital Salang Pass tunnel. The paratroopers, reinforced to over a division in strength, moved out from the Kabul airport perimeter to seize the capital. *Spetsnaz* special forces, having positioned themselves before the invasion, took headquarters, airfields, communi-cations centres, and other key points.

A *spetsnaz* attempt to neutralize Amin failed; reportedly spearheaded by KGB *spetsnaz* units, linking up with men inside the palace, it lost the element of surprise when its commander was inadvertently shot by his own men. The Soviets may have wanted Amin alive, but most probably he was more convenient dead. It required a two-battalion attack by BMD-mounted paratroopers to take the Duralamin Palace. In the fighting, Lieutenant-General Viktor Paputin—head of the uniformed armed forces of the Soviet Ministry of the Interior and a Brezhnev protégé—ended up dead, the cause variously rumoured as falling at the head of his troops while storming the Darulaman Palace to suicide in remorse that a hard-fought battle had been needed.

Amin was promptly executed by his erstwhile allies and replaced by the *Parcham* leader Babrak Karmal (flown in from Tashkent where he had been in exile) as quisling Prime Minister. He stopped *en route* to make his first radio broadcast from the Soviet Union.

As 1979 ended, the Soviets could commend themselves for a successful example of operational level force projection, as in Czechoslovakia in 1968. Political surprise had been achieved despite extended mobilization. The United States had once again shown it could not do much to block Soviet aims. Airborne forces, special operations forces, advisers, and fifth columnists had pre-empted organized DRA resistance in a way that would have received high marks at the Voroshilov General Staff Academy. But the new year was to bring a new war.

1980

The Soviets apparently hoped that, as in Hungary in 1956 or Czechoslovakia in 1968, the replacing of one Communist ruler by another, plus the provision of an army of occupation, would bring tranquillity. The return of *Parcham* to power meant that all the excesses of 1978–9 could be blamed on Amin. On Soviet advice, the regime's anti-Islamic campaign was abruptly dropped and, as in Soviet Central Asia, a show of respect for religion was to be made. The *Khalq* leadership was purged, but they retained cabinet positions and influence in the military. But this restored peace within the ranks of the PDPA only temporarily; it did nothing to restoring peace in Afghanistan.

Crumbling even before the Soviet invasion, in 1980 the Kabul regime army fell through desertion to a strength of 20,000. Early in the new year, fighting broke out between DRA garrisons, around Kabul, and the Soviets. The 8th Division at Qargha fought a brief but bitter action with Soviet paratroops before most of it melted away into the mountains. An Afghan airborne battalion resisted disarming by the Soviets, but this time troops loyal to the Kabul regime were used to clean them out.

This fighting, plus a number of mass defections in the Kunar Valley and Nangarhar province, forced the Soviets into a quick re-evaluation. Their original plan of clearing out the guerrillas with a series of large sweeps by Kabul regime units was not going to work. The Soviets would have to do the fighting themselves, but they had found their own motorized rifle divisions, the bulk composed of reservists, to be inept troops. Many of them were poorly trained Muslims, more interested in finishing their time and going home.

Strikes and demonstrations spread through the cities; Kandahar flared into open warfare on 1 January and parties of Soviets who had left the perimeter around the airfield were hacked to pieces. In Kabul, 21 February saw the anti-Soviet uprising of 'The Night of "Allah Akbar"' (the traditional Muslim warcry), with rioting following a general strike staged by shopkeepers and workers. Hundreds were shot by the police; Soviet helicopters and Kabul regime troops attacked at dawn, leaving at least 300 dead. Many of the 5,000 arrested were later executed.

During further Kabul demonstrations, the DRA Army refused to open fire and the Soviets moved in to gun down rioters, leading to the spread of mutinies which started around Kabul and in the Kunar, and reached Ghazni by May. Throughout the spring, repeated demonstrations by students were met by Soviet gunfire, those in April leaving more than 200 dead. The north saw widespread resistance, especially in Badakhshan (where the provincial capital was briefly occupied) and Takhar.

Right: In 1980, Soviet tanks went into action without motorized rifle support on several occasions and suffered considerable losses despite the lack of Resistance anti-tank weapons. Some Resistance groups evolved sophisticated anti-tank tactics quickly, while others relied on heroic and costly measures. Most learned to let the tanks roll by and wait for the replenishment supplies to arrive and attack them. (Committee for a Free Afghanistan)

The Soviets replied with a series of large-scale ground sweeps conducted by mechanized combined arms forces, but without much skill or imagination, into the Kunar valley in February, March, May, September and November. The latter, against the Sukhurod region, featured large-scale destruction of agriculture. July saw the first large-scale use of the surface-scattered PFM-1 'butterfly' mines. Throughout Afghanistan, more Hind gunship and Hip transport helicopters made their presence felt, the symbols of the new masters of Kabul.

A Soviet combined arms force moved into Paktia in March and suffered heavy losses, one particular motorized rifle battalion being badly cut up. One company, isolated, blazed away from its APCs until its ammunition was exhausted and, with nightfall, the Afghans moved in.

The systematic destruction of agriculture near Kabul started in June. Soviet and Kabul regime forces tried, unsuccessfully, to expand their perimeter at Bamiyan in July–August, but were defeated by Sayid Jaglan (another army officer who had joined the Resistance) and, more significantly, a broad range of Hazara forces. The Ghazni area was swept in May and June and Wardak province in November—the latter a hard-fought but ultimately successful operation involving elements of several divisions. The first Soviet offensives into the Panjshir Valley, where Ahmad Shah Massoud had now established himself as leader, were in April and September–October, but they fared no better than the two 1979 offensives by Kabul regime troops.

In response to condemnation of the invasion by the United Nations General Assembly, the Non-Aligned Movement, and the Organization of Islamic Nations, the Soviets started the diplomatic activity that would continue throughout the war. They stated repeatedly that they would withdraw their forces as soon as the foreign influence which was imperilling the Kabul regime ceased (they had told their troops, before the invasion, that it was Pakistani and Israeli mercenaries, led by CIA agents, that troubled Afghanistan). The Soviets staged a withdrawal of those forces not required for counter-insurgency warfare—brigades of heavy artillery and surface-to-air missiles, plus a tank regiment. At the end of the year, however, they increased their forces' strength, bringing in more motorized rifle divisions.

The seven major Sunni resistance parties, installed in Peshawar, Pakistan, attempted to organize a unified front. These efforts (which had started before the Soviet invasion), despite the attempted calling of a Loya Jirga in Pakistan, had little real success. The differences between the Peshawar leadership and those actually fighting inside Afghanistan started to emerge. Foreign aid started to flow with the Democrat administration in Washington funding a limited flow of arms. Pakistan now found itself confronted not only with a security dilemma, but with a huge cross-border influx of refugees.

Above: A Hind attacks. Because they always work in mutual support, firing at a Hind as it passes overhead while attacking is likely to expose one's position to the Hind's wingman. Because of their night vision equipment, they were able to attack at night without the use of flares. (US Information Agency)

Below: T-54A '517', captured by the Resistance, was committed to the three-tank attack on Urgun in December 1983, which failed. It represented the most extensive Resistance use of tanks during the war up until that point. '517' is also the tank which accidentally ran over an Australian cameraman while he was filming, the second Western journalist killed in the war. (Committee for a Free Afghanistan)

Right: The actions of the Soviets towards the civilian population were fundamentally different from those of Western armies in similar counter-insurgency situations. This has been reflected by a refugee population that has shaped the course of the war and is the result of Soviet de-population efforts. In the mid-1980s, 75 per cent of the total in Pakistan were women and children. (US Information Agency)

1981

This year saw a shift away from Soviet sweeps to smaller operations as a reaction to the heavy casualties which the 1980 offensives had yielded; air bombardment became more regular and intense.

The 1981 ground offensives were mostly aimed at improving the security of major bases and Kabul—stressing maximum Kabul regime participation—and they proved disappointing. One offensive in Logar in April was a guerrilla victory; another offensive against Paghman, north of Kabul, in July fared no better. The Panjshir offensives in April and September, the June–July offensive in the Tora Bora area of Nangrahar, and the October offensive in Kandahar failed to yield results, although the latter two led to widespread de-population and destruction of agriculture.

The 'non-party' National Fatherland Front (still existing in 1988 as the National Front) was inaugurated by Karmal. It was intended to serve a purpose similar to those that had appeared in eastern Europe after the Second World War, i.e., to assist in the transition to Communist rule. It could not however attract much support beyond the small numbers that were already willing to support the PDPA.

Outside aid for the Resistance continued, but at a relatively limited level; while the first private voluntary organizations to aim their relief efforts inside Afghanistan started operations.

1982

In 1982, with the Kabul regime army still of limited usefulness in offensive combat, the Soviets continued to do most of the fighting. They reverted to large-scale ground sweeps, combined with helicopter-mobile operations to encircle Resistance strongholds.

Initially, this led to success: a winter offensive in Parwan, in January, surrounded

Above: By late 1982, the Resistance were getting more weapons such as this RPG-7. (Committee for a Free Afghanistan)

SOVIET OPERATIONS, 1980–1: A VIEW FROM THE RESISTANCE

'Soviet troops, in the spring and summer of 1980, moved in heavy columns along the major roads. Closely supported by aircraft and helicopter gunships, these columns found comfort in technical superiority. Obsessed by massive firepower to supporting the advance, they fired to the front and flanks (sometimes at random) to suppress suspected *mujahideen* positions. The lack of troop patrols and the absence of tactical reconnaissance and security elements, especially on the ridges and high ground that so often dominated the roads, was exploited by the *mujahideen*, who on several occasions launched successful ambushes, despite being deployed where they could have been easily outflanked and routed. The inexperienced Soviet troops would not dismount and resort to close combat. Firepower could not produce results because it was not exploited by attack at close quarters. The *mujahideen*, short of weapons, often defeated totally mechanized Soviet forces, unable to operate effectively in the rugged and close terrain where the guerrillas moved. In 1980, Soviet forces were unsupported by light infantry.'

'1981 modifications proved an inadequate solution. Mechanized forces leap-frogged between fire bases 15–20km apart (the range of most artillery, including the BM-21 MRLs). Before they advanced, preparatory barrages would be fired, sometimes for several hours, supplemented by aircraft and helicopter gunships. This enabled the ground forces to move rapidly between the bases, but the *mujahideen* could still outmanoeuvre the enemy so as to harass successfully the columns during their march.'

Lieutenant Colonel Ali Ahmad Jalali, Ph.D., psc
(a *mujahideen* commander at that time).

and annihilated much of the resistance in that province. Similar offensives took place near Kandahar and Herat. In the Logar valley, south of Kabul, the Soviets had started de-populating along the main Kabul–Gardez highway in 1981, and followed this with a two-stage offensive in June and September, 1982, which twinned heliborne operations with combined arms columns to destroy many resistance groups.

The Panjshir V (April–May) and Panjshir VI (September) offensives were two of the biggest battles of the war. Sweeps targeted areas that could be used to support guerrilla attacks on Kabul. Two offensives in June and October left Paghman desolate (though it has never been fully cleared). Between the two, however, a counter-attack defeated the Kabul regime forces and cadres that were holding the area. Large-scale offensives were made in Wardak province; the Laghman Valley, east of Kabul (November), and the Ghorband Valley, north of Kabul (May).

Elsewhere, Kabul regime forces spearheaded a number of offensives in peripheral areas, including those around Ghazni (May), the foothills of Farah province (April), and Mazar-e-Sharif (April); Paktia province, however, remained the Kabul regime's headache. An understrength Kabul regime division's attempted drive to the Pakistani border in April triggered one of the first co-ordinated multi-party Resistance actions and led to the near-destruction of the Communist column.

Resistance offensive action had increased throughout 1982; raids on Kabul and other targets continued, cutting power supplies in December. An explosion, possibly accidental, in the Salang Pass tunnel in October caused hundreds of casualties.

1983

Starting in late 1982, but becoming apparent in 1983, the Soviets adopted an 'air war' approach with extensive bombing of villages, to de-populate vital areas, combined with heliborne operations and ground sweeps. This may have been a response to the failure of the two Panjshir offensives (the Panjshir V offensive inflicted only 10 per cent losses on Massoud's fighting men) in 1982, and the realization that many of the ground offensives had led to casualties without long-term gain.

The problem of dealing with the Panjshir was resolved for a year; a truce was concluded with Massoud in March, allowing him to focus his energies outside the valley for the first time and to organize throughout Dari-speaking Afghanistan.

Kandahar city, with large areas under Resistance control, was subject to extensive bombing before a Soviet–DRA attack in March. Herat city was effectively occupied by the Resistance in April and the resulting Soviet counter-attack included the use of

heavy bombers against the city itself.

The Soviets continued to make combined arms offensives: one into Logar in January 1983 being particularly successful while one around Ghazni in June was not. Throughout central Afghanistan, Communist-held positions – including Kabul – were repeatedly attacked and road ambushes became more and more frequent. The increased flow of arms aid, starting in late 1982, and the slowly improving Resistance effectiveness was apparent by 1983. A Resistance offensive in Paktia and Paktika provinces in the summer and autumn scored victories over Kabul regime forces at Jadji and Khost, with a commando battalion being totally destroyed in one encounter and a nest of tribal militia ('Little Moscow') cleaned out in another, forcing the Kabul regime back into their garrisons in the border area. In December the fort at Urgun was besieged.

1984

The emphasis on air operations was carried into the new year, but applied with more intensity. New, more aggressive combined-arms tactics, including the expanded use of heliborne special operations forces, were seen in January, when a Soviet force relieved Urgun. A successful Panjshiri large-scale ambush by guerrillas on the Salang Pass highway in March was followed, in April, by the Panjshir VII offensive, aimed at desolating the valley. By June, Massoud was back in the upper reaches of the main Panjshir valley. The Soviets kept their troops in the lower valley until, after launching the Panjshir VIII offensive in September, the garrisons were turned over to Kabul regime troops.

In June sequential multi-division offensives were launched near Herat and Kandahar. Using heavy air support, both aimed systematically to destroy the major approaches to the cities and led to fighting more intense than that in the Panjshir.

In July–August, the Logar and Shomali valleys were swept, followed by renewed fighting near Herat. In August–October, Soviet forces relieved the besieged fort at Ali Khel in Paktia, coupled with increased

Right: The fruits of victory: 1987. Ahmad Shah Massoud (right) examines a 76.2mm field gun captured by his forces at Kalafghan in July 1987. Each of Massoud's victories has yielded a small but varied collection of light artillery and mortars, as these weapons are frequently dispersed in Kabul regime garrisons. None of the garrisons taken by Massoud in 1986–8 have been re-established by the regime. (Afghan Media Resource Centre, Peshawar)

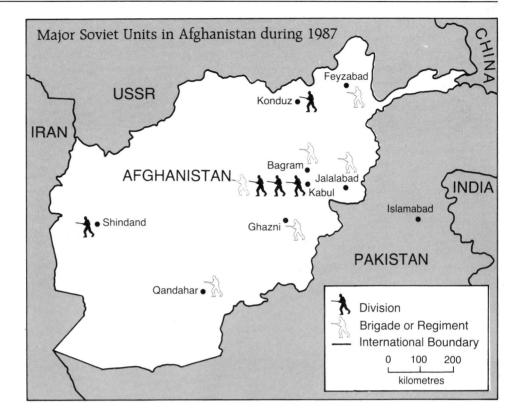

Major Soviet Units in Afghanistan during 1987

efforts to seal the border with Pakistan. Paghman was again hit by a Soviet offensive in late 1984.

Despite persistent Soviet offensives the guerrillas continued to strike near Kabul, introducing 107mm and 122mm rockets to the war. Power lines between Kabul and the Sarubi dam were destroyed in August. SA-7s began to become more numerous but were still not supplied in adequate numbers.

PANJSHIR VII

The Panjshir VII offensive, which opened on 21 April 1984, followed Soviet attempts to renew the year-old ceasefire with Ahmad Shah Massoud. When Massoud learnt of the Soviet preparations for an offensive, he moved to pre-empt them. His *motareks* (full-time fighting men' of the Panjshir) launched a devastating ambush of a fuel convoy along the Salang Highway in March, which caused a severe fuel shortage in Kabul. The guerillas had extensive warning of the attack, from their sympathizers in the Kabul regime forces. After consulting with local leaders and the religious figures, Massoud decided not to fight, but to side-step the Soviet blow; civilians and the bulk of the fighting forces pulled out of the main valley at its mouth, some 70km north of Kabul. After supervising widespread mining of the main valley, Massoud himself also withdrew into the surrounding mountains, which rise to a height of over 4,000m.

Soviet reinforcements were flown in for the big offensive – 6,000 troops, including a regiment of the crack 104th Guards Airborne Division from Kirovabad. Most of the 20,000 Soviet troops that took part in the Panjshir VII offensive were paratroops. The regiment from the 104th Guards Airborne was committed to battle, as was the 375th Guards Airborne Regiment from the now disbanded 105th Guards Airborne Division and much (including two full regiments) of the 103rd Guards Airborne Division, based at Kabul. The Kabul-based 108th Motorized Rifle Division also contributed a regiment.

The Kabul regime's army contributed 6,000 troops to Panjshir VII, including: tribal militia; columns drawn from the 8th and 20th Divisions; and 38th Commando Brigade, considered one of the best Kabul regime units, which suffered several hundred desertions before it could enter the Panjshir. This was apparently due to the fact that, because of its supposed reliability, the 38th Commando Brigade had been used as a 'fire brigade', the Kabul regime's mobile reserve, for the past year. It was filled with green replacements – mostly disaffected conscripts, including young boys and old men kidnapped off the streets, – as well as tired veterans. Thirty-six TU-16 Badger and a larger number of Su-24 Fencer bombers deployed to Mary and Termez in the Soviet Union, reflecting the fact that, since 1984 the Soviet war in Afghanistan has become more and more of an air war. They had the task of destroying the will and ability of the Afghan people to resist, by producing more intensive air bombardments than on the large-scale cordon-and-sweep operations of 1980 or 1982.

Soviet command and control preparations were also extensive. A forward command post was set up of the size normally associated with an independent army-level operation. A representative of the General Staff reportedly arrived from Moscow to provide high-level direction. A four-engined An-12 Cub, configured as an airborne command post, was dubbed 'the flying Kremlin' by the Kabul regime troops.

This concentration of force was not carried out peacefully, and on 20 April Massoud, having evacuated the main valley, launched a spoiling attack on assembly areas near Anawa, at the mouth of the valley.

The offensive was preceded by extensive high-level carpet bombing by Badgers, starting on 20 April. However, this was not wholly successful, and at least one Badger flew into a mountain while on a bombing run. Poor weather rendered the Fencers ineffective.

Part of the preparation was an attempted assassination of Massoud, but the assassin selected by the KGB and KHAD was a Panjshiri double agent, who promptly turned the 23 members of his support team and their contacts over to the Resistance.

On 21 April, beginning with a rolling artillery barrage, the Soviet forces crossed the line of departure and started ebbing up the valley. They reached the ruins of Rokha on 24 April, and then Khenj, the immediate objective, where the main column halted. The Soviets repeated their tactic, used in the Panjshir V offensive in 1982, of using helicopter-inserted 'stop groups' forward of their armoured spearheads. In the second phase of the offensive, heliborne battalion-sized assaults were made at Dasht-e-Rawat and the entrance to the main side valley. This provoked the heaviest fighting of the battle. One of the heliborne battalions, moving beyond artillery range, suffered at the hands of rapidly concentrating guerrillas and had to call in heavy airstrikes. On 2 May, Soviet bombers caught at least one guerrilla group moving in the open in the main valley, and inflicted heavy losses.

In another part of the second phase of the operation, starting in early May, the Soviets tried to apply their tactics of having separate columns converge on an objective, while other forces were landed by helicopter inside the cordon. The Soviets moved into the valleys adjoining the Panjshir. A separate column moving from Khinjan, on the Salang Pass highway on the north slope of the Hindu Kush into the Andarab Valley, linked up with another heliborne forward detachment. There was considerable fighting. Other Soviet forces, moving from Jalalabad, moved up to the Alishang and Kantiwar Passes, the southern approaches to the Panjshir. Militia forces moved down the Anjuman Valley towards the Panjshir. Other forces moved out of the main valley to move slowly up the Khenj, Hazara and Bazarak side valleys. In the Khenj valley, a Kabul regime army unit (its strength put at 900 by the Resistance), switched sides. Meanwhile, in the main valley Kabul regime forces dug in at Anawa, Rokha, and Bazarak. The Soviets provided both the hammer and the anvil, but they never brought Massoud to the decisive battle they had obviously prepared to win.

While there was fighting in the side valleys (and the Communists did not long maintain a presence in many of them), most of the guerrilla action in the Panjshir was in the form of hit-and-run raids, launched from the surrounding mountains. Massoud was reinforced by other Afghans who had heard of the offensive, one group coming from Wardak province, south of Kabul. To relieve the pressure on the Panjshir, other Afghans launched attacks on Communist positions near Kabul and Jalalabad. Massoud was still able to strike outside the valley. An Afghan raid on the large Bagram airbase in May destroyed several MiG-21 Fishbeds on the ground.

This was an impressive and well-coordinated offensive, apart from the relatively high loss rate of helicopters and the defeat of one Soviet heliborne battalion. But, on the whole, despite committing many of their best troops, overall Soviet performance was doubtlessly disappointing. They failed to capture Massoud or defeat any sizable Resistance forces, which had pulled back before the offensive.

The failure to make headway into the side valleys is understandable. Airpower had proven of limited effectiveness, especially against the narrow side valleys. Most of these valleys are narrow and wind, making it impossible to get helicopters or armoured vehicles into them, and providing ideal terrain for ambushes. By May, the remainder of the Badgers had returned to their normal bases of Bobriusk and Tartu.

The Soviets did not withdraw totally when they started pulling their forces out towards the end of June, but brought in Kabul regime forces to hold forts constructed as far up the valley as Pechgour, which was to be the scene of fighting until its fall in 1987. By the end of June Massoud was back in the Panjshir, starting the usual raids and attacks on Soviet positions in the main valley and attacking their resupply convoys. The Soviets did not defeat Massoud or break his forces, and diplomatic sources in Kabul reported total Soviet casualties of at least 500; the Resistance estimated 200 dead.

The Soviets tried again with the Panjshir VIII offensive in September. This was a series of smaller, battalion-sized, largely heliborne attacks into the upper valley. While it gained some initial success, it did not prevent Massoud from regaining his position throughout the north, and passing day-to-day control of the Panjshir to Mahmood Khan.

1985

1985 opened with the PDPA's 20th anniversary celebrations in Kabul being disrupted by a 107mm rocket barrage underlining the fact that the PDPA had not even 'built socialism in one city'. As a result, the Kabul defences were strengthened, a move that continues to consume, in 1988, a large percentage of overall Communist resources and has tied down a significant amount of Soviet and Kabul regime strength. The defensive perimeter was expanded to cover most potential 107mm rocket-firing positions. Three lines of outposts and checkpoints were established, and by 1987, the Soviets had secured relative security and quiet inside the capital itself.

In 1985, Soviet artillery and rocket-launchers supplemented aircraft to achieve de-population through firepower, an approach mandated by the continued weakness of Kabul regime forces. Real improvement could be seen in KHAD, however, the Kabul regime secret police and a *de facto* arm of the KGB. The stock of its chief, Najibullah, continued to rise and he became recognized as Karmal's heir apparent.

An increasing emphasis on interdiction was seen throughout 1985. Aid to the guerrillas was coming inside in increasing strength, which lead the Soviets to try to increase their efforts to disrupt the flow of supplies from Pakistan.

Interdiction was also in mind when the Kunar Valley, scene of much hard fighting dating back to early 1979, was again circled in red pencil on Soviet situation maps. An attempt by Kabul regime units to relieve the besieged garrison at Barikot in Kunar, at the north end of the valley, was defeated in January–February. A second push in May–June succeeded in getting a relief column through.

This campaign was not limited to the Pakistani frontier; an offensive near Herat in the summer may have been aimed at isolating the area from Iran. Another offensive in the Logar Valley, aimed at cutting the main route from the Pakistan border to the north of Afghanistan, involved extensive use of special operations forces and was marked by massacres of Afghan civilians.

The destruction of rural agriculture was the goal of offensives in Laghman and in the Helmand Valley. Until then, the Helmand Valley had not been attacked, but following Resistance attacks on outposts near the Helmand Valley Dam (built with American aid in the 1960s), a Soviet combined arms offensive, again making extensive use of special operations forces, rolled in and

1985 – SECOND KUNAR OFFENSIVE

While the first Kunar offensive of 1985 failed to yield lasting results, planning for the second offensive was probably soon under way, possibly even before the first one ended. The first had not succeeded in reaching the besieged garrison in Barikot, but had reinforced the Kabul regime garrisons in the southern part of the Kunar. While the first offensive had drawn heavy Afghan resistance, the Soviets realized that if the guerrillas concentrated to oppose another offensive, they would become excellent targets for airpower.

Soviet high-level command posts were set up at Jalalabad, as was the forward command post of the Kabul regime's I Corps. Elements of 11th and 9th Infantry Divisions of the Kabul regime, deployed in the area with headquarters at Jalalabad and Chagha Sarai, had provided most of the manpower for the first offensive and would be called upon to do so again. This time they were reinforced by the 37th and 38th Commando brigades, two infantry regiments from other divisions, one border brigade, and militia forces. The Soviets contributed, in addition to aircraft, one motorized rifle regiment, a brigade or regiment sized airborne-air assault force, and at least one *spetsnaz* battalion. Total strength was more than 10,000 men.

Planning was thorough. The immediate mission was to recover the same ground as the first Kunar offensive: to open the main Jalalabad–Chagha Sarai road, establish flank security posts and block major Resistance supply routes. The subsequent mission of the operation was what the first Kunar offensive had been unable to accomplish: the destruction of the Resistance strongholds in the Pech Dara, Asmar and Barikot areas and, ultimately, to relieve Barikot.

The offensive started before dawn on 23 May. The Jalalabad–Chagha Sarai highway was opened. Inserted, in many cases, by Soviet helicopters, outposts of light forces, militia and border troops reinforced by fire bases were established along the flanks. Once this had been done, the long combined-arms column moved forward. Once Chagha Sarai was reached, the headquarters and heavy artillery were brought up, the troops went into an assembly area, and the Soviets troops were pulled in from the outposts, leaving them to regime forces.

The second phase of the operation was launched with a secondary attack towards Pech Dara and a main attack up the valley towards Asmar. Both thrusts were preceded by air assaults on the crests overlooking the route of advance. The Pech Dara thrust soon bogged down; the initial Soviet move had given the Resistance time to bring in reinforcements. The column advancing towards Pech Dara was unable to link up with the heliborne forward detachments inserted along its route of advance, which had now become the targets of the guerrilla attack. The Soviets, mainly tough paratroopers, fought back hard, and at least one Hero of the Soviet Union medal was earned, but they suffered heavy casualties and had to be evacuated by helicopter, at least one squad being left behind.

The main column ground slowly north through the Kunar Valley, advancing on a one-tank frontage, encountering heavy defences in the Narai area. Spetsnaz forces were inserted deep into Resistance-held areas. Other Soviet special forces were used to seize key points on the hills overlooking the column, but were withdrawn by helicopters at night only to be redeployed the next day. Militia forces were used for flank security. Communist fighter-bombers and attack helicopters flew 150 sorties per day in support. The Resistance withdrew in face of heavy columns supported by heavy artillery fire and air strikes, only to attack in small groups against the enemy supply lines and on enemy bases at night. As the main column neared Barikot, a Soviet battalion was lifted by helicopter into the perimeter, following extensive airstrikes against the guerrillas surrounding the fort, and launched a break-out attack against heavy resistance down the valley to meet the advancing column. Losses were heavy on both sides.

By the middle of June the Resistance had fired off most of its ammunition, especially that for 107mm rockets and RPG-7 anti-tank rocket-launchers, and pulled back. The Soviet column reached the Barikot, where they stayed for only a few hours before again moving back down the valley, to Chagha Serai, and Asmar.

As with most conventional offensives in guerrilla warfare the operation's impact was short-lived, and the Soviet units were soon withdrawn to Kabul and Jalalabad. Throughout the summer the Resistance eliminated the isolated posts that had been established following the offensive, and again besieged Barikot and Asmar.

inflicted heavy losses.

In the north, Massoud had started to operate more often away from the Panjshir. He held the first Council of the North in 1984, gathering together a broad range of commanders. After the death of Zabioullah, the major commander in the Mazar-e-Sharif area, in late 1984, Massoud's influence expanded. In the Panjshir itself, despite the summer Panjshir IX offensive, this time emphasizing heliborne forces, Massoud still controlled the upper main valley.

Jalulladin Haqani emerged as the regional leader in southern Paktia and Paktika provinces, which were the main focus of operations during the summer of 1985. In Paktia, the Soviets' long-term headache, the Resistance, had used the influx of weaponry to increase the intensity of two long-running sieges of Kabul regime-manned fortresses, Ali Khel and Khost. At Khost, defended by a brigade-sized division reinforced by strong militia units, the Resistance tried to fight their way through the outposts on the hills

1985 – SECOND PAKTIA OFFENSIVE

The second major offensive of 1985, in Paktia, was intended to first isolate and destroy large *mujahideen* strongholds in Azra, Jadji, Chamkani, and around Khost; second, to relieve the siege of Ali Khel in Paktia; third, to interdict infiltration and supply routes; and fourth, to raise the siege of Khost, opening the roads blocked for years by the Resistance.

Following standard Soviet practice, the offensive had both an immediate and a subsequent objective. The immediate objective was to isolate Azra, using converging columns, followed by the destruction in detail of the *mujahideen* in Azra, Jadji and Chamkani and the relief of Ali Khel. Forces would close the main supply routes along the Kurram valley from Pakistan. The subsequent objective was the relief of Khost, again from multiple directions, both from the north and the west (from Gardez). The *mujahideen* supply routes south of Khost were also to be cut, especially those running through Zhawar, stronghold of Jalulladin

Haqani the foremost Resistance commander in Paktia.

Even by Soviet Army standards, it was a sizeable operation, conducted in an area stretching from Kabul to the Pakistan border, over a sector 100km wide and 200km deep. The 15,000 or more Communist troops included two or three Soviet regiments – motorized rifle or airborne – reinforced with air assault, reconnaissance, and *spetsnaz* units. The Kabul regime provided its III Corps, with forces from the 11th, 12th and 25th Divisions, reinforced by one regiment each from the 7th and 8th Divisions, elements of 1st, 2nd, and 8th Border Brigades, the 203rd Reconnaissance Battalion, 37th and 38th Commando Brigades and the 466th Commando Battalion from Kandahar. Strong militia forces were also to be used, both from Paktia and those brought in from other provinces.

After lengthy preparation (including tactical airlifts into Gardez and Khost), the main Communist columns started out on 21 August. The complex plan saw combined arms columns attacking simultaneously along Kabul–Logar (jumping off from the main Kabul–Gardez road), Hisurak (jumping off from Jalalabad), Khagroni and Wasiri–Azra axes against the bases in the mountains near Azra south-east of Kabul. The attack was preceded by heavy air and artillery bombardment. Massacres of civilians at Khurd Kabul, Logar and later in Azra were apparently intended to encourage guerrillas to suspend fighting and move their families across the border to Pakistan. The main column headed toward the border through Logar, advancing 20–25km daily, and reached Gardez on 26 August.

Once the combined-arms forces had successfully thrown a cordon across the major routes running into Azra, the Soviets made a series of air assaults throughout the area. Some of these were by a force of several battalions of Soviet airborne or air assault units, others by Afghan militia. The fighting lasted five days, with the Resistance unable to reinforce due to the Soviet cordon. After destroying a number of villages and dispersing much of the Resistance, the Communist forces were heli-lifted out. Meanwhile, Ali Khel fort was resupplied.

Preceded by a road-opening detachment with large numbers of engineers and mine-clearing equipment following the usual air and artillery preparation, the main Communist column launched its thrust from Gardez towards Jadji as soon as it arrived at the jumping off point, late on 26 August. As the column passed the Said Karan valley and reached Du Soraka it encountered stiff opposition and in fierce fighting suffered heavy losses in personnnel and equipment. The column now divided into two forces, intending to make a co-ordinated drive on the Pakistani border, one pushing towards Jadji and the other towards Chamkani, to destroy the Resistance strongholds in that area. Meanwhile, as the Soviets advanced, more Resistance reinforcements arrived and the proximity to Pakistan brought many out of the refugee camps and thereby reduced guerilla logistical problems. The Soviet thrust ground to a halt in the face of increasing *mujahideen* resistance. It was obvious that the Soviets could not get to Khost or to the border without prohibitive losses, so they retreated, pulling back to Gardez on 10 September. The forces still operating in Azra and surrounding areas were aliso withdrawn.

But while this battle was going on, the Soviets opened another front, near Khost. Two or three battalions of paratroopers and three Kabul regime regiments had been flown into Khost. Throughout the war the Soviets would fly in such units to an encircled area and then make a break-out attack. These fresh forces provided those within the Khost perimeter, forced on to the defensive throughout the summer, with the capability to go over to the offensive. They launched their breakout attack, aimed at Zhawar and the other Resistance bases and supply routes in the Zadran area. Despite strong air support, the advance was slow, as Resistance reinforcements moved to the sound of the guns. Although by 11 September the Soviet spearhead had penetrated to within 1,000m of Zhawar, their initial objective, casualties mounted and again the order was given for withdrawal. By the end of the month, the offensive was over, its objectives unattained.

Despite their heavy losses, the Resistance had won a battlefield victory. Philippe Flandrine a French journalist on the scene, reported: 'The *mujahideen* were organized in groups of 25 and 30, very calm, disciplined and professional. They won a victory by defending their position well and by preventing the enemy from reaching Zhawar. The enemy troops cannot do better; they will have to retreat to their bases in Khost or suffer increasingly heavy losses. A strong offensive was pushed back. The *mujahideen* learned something and will become harder. The Soviets must also be drawing some depressing conclusions.'

Above: General Mikhail M. Zaitsev. Appointed, by Gorbachev, to command the Southern TVD High Command in mid-1985, this up-and-coming general (then a youthful 62) was given 1-2 years to deliver a successful military solution. Following the pyrrhic victory of Zhawar, he was unable to deliver and Gorbachev began to move for a political settlement. (US Department of Defense)

overlooking the airfield. Backed by Soviet airstrikes, the Kabul regime grimly held on. In response to these Resistance attacks, a major Soviet offensive was launched into Paktia, but succeeded only in relieving Ali Khel.

1986

The winter of 1985–6 was marked by Soviet efforts to instigate a trans-border raising of Pathan tribes; Afridi, Shin-wari and Hill Mohmands were supposed to embarrass the Pakistani Government and cut Resistance supply lines on both sides of the border. The loyalty did not last, however, but helped raise the political pressure on the Pakistanis, as did the first major offensive of 1986.

The Soviets were continuing their interdiction efforts of 1985, but were trying to create the appearance of a Kabul regime with independent operational capability. Large Communist forces advanced to the Pakistani border as part of a major offensive that destroyed Zhawar, the base of Jalluladin Haqani. This, the most significant offensive of 1986, proved a pyrrhic victory and may have been the impetus for Gorbachev to move towards a diplomatic solution although it seemed a signal success at the time.

Other border offensives in early 1986 were launched by Kabul regime forces around Herat and Soviet forces in Faryab

province. A Kabul regime offensive in January in the Naizan Valley of Nangarhar, however, failed to carry out its mission, and in November, the Soviet 66th Motorized Rifle Brigade from Jalalabad was sent back in, leading to a series of hard battles against well-armed guerrillas.

Soviet offensives around Kabul continued, one into the Logar Valley in August encountering massed use of SA-7 SAMs. In the north, the Soviets made gains in undercutting the Resistance around Mazar-e-Sharif and in economically tying the region to the Soviet Union. Mazar was the site of many Soviet construction projects, which continued to suggest a long-term presence. A Soviet advance along the Kunduz–Faizabad highway was blunted by a multi-party Resistance force in March.

To counter these Soviet actions in the north, Massoud started his campaign to build the infrastructure, politically and physically, for a campaign that he foresaw might take a generation. He staged a number of offensive operations outside the Panjshir, raiding Bagram airfield, the Salang Pass highway, and, most significantly, taking the Kabul regime garrison at Fakhar by a well-planned assault. He now deployed several 120-man units of the Central Forces, of whom only a minority were Panjshiri. Paid a salary and able to fight anywhere in the north, they were the first true Resistance manoeuvre units. Before this, only the nearest group to each garrison would attack, and this could usually not amount to more than harassment. Massoud could now concentrate forces against the most important garrisons and take them.

Early 1986 probably saw the high-water mark of Soviet special forces operations. The interdiction efforts around Kandahar were particularly effective early in the year, but, by the end of the year their effectiveness, which had so challenged the Resistance in 1984–5, had apparently decreased.

Politically, the Gorbachev era started to affect Afghanistan, with the fall of Babrak Karmal and the emergence of Najibullah (known as Najib in recent years, single names being common in Afghanistan), who consolidated his position as the strong man in Kabul and First Secretary of the PDPA. The switch in power took place in May, and

by November Karmal had lost all his government and party posts.

The calling of a new pro-Communist *Loya Jirga* and the emergence of a 'National Reconciliation' policy to bolster the National Fatherland Front as a tool to increase the Kabul Regime's minimal support showed an attempt to revitalize Soviet political strategy, but once again they met with little success. A limited Soviet troop withdrawal – six regiments, mainly air defence, in October – was also aimed at an external audience.

Talk of a Soviet withdrawal had started within days of the invasion, and had increased with the 1980 troop withdrawal. It had increased again with the strategy of the indirect negotiations between the Kabul Regime and Pakistan in 1982. The Soviets have always said that they wanted to leave; they simply want to win first. But after Gorbachev's Vladivostok speech in June 1986 and the ambiguous treatment of Afghanistan in his 'bleeding wound' speech at that year's Party Congress in Moscow, the possibility of a real change in Soviet Afghan policy was raised for the first time.

The most significant single battlefield event of 1986 took place in Nangarhar Province on 26 September: three out of four Soviet helicopters in a formation were destroyed in quick succession by US-made heat-seeking man-portable Stinger surface-

Above: 1986: this up-armoured T-62E main battle tank of the 'Berlin' Tank Regiment, 5th Guards Motorized Rifle division, based near Shindand, is leaving Afghanistan as part of the publicized sham withdrawal announced by Gorbachev in Vladivostok. (US Department of Defense)

ARGHANDAB

Kandahar has always been bandit country to the Soviets. Despite the numerous offensives and repeated bombings and shellings in the relatively flat terrain, the Resistance has not been defeated though much of the once fertile agricultural land around the city has been laid waste.

Kandahar was one of the traditional crossroads of southern Asia – Alexander the Great let his elephants wallow there before advancing to cross the Indus – it has a diverse and cosmopolitan population, although primarily Pathan and Sunni Muslim. This is reflected in diversity of resistance parties there. To reduce friction, a rotating leadership between parties exists, under leaders such as Mullah Nakib, Lala Malang and Abdul Latif, not dominated by a single leader or party. The Kandahar leaders are strong, forceful men, better at battle than at organization and institution building.

In early 1987, using their new weapons – 107mm Chinese-made rocket-launchers, covered by Stinger SAMs – the Resistance attacked the Soviet positions at Peshmul and Hassangay and the Kandahar city WAD headquarters. But the object was not to take these positions. Rather, it was to limit Soviet interference in the real target of the offensive: the Kabul regime militia forces which held the outposts that constituted the Communist outer defences around Kandahar. Three of the independent militias were especially targeted: those loyal to Ismatullah, a former Kabul regime officer turned Resistance commander turned militia leader; that of Meri Baluchis, who had crossed the border from Pakistan in the 1970s, and that of Uzbeks from Jowzjan. These all suffered heavy losses.

In response, in the last week of May, the Soviets launched an offensive against Resistance strongholds in the Arghandab district, 10km outside Kandahar. Most of the 6,000 troops committed to the offensive were Afghan, from the local 15th Division, and 7th Tank Brigade reinforced with columns from the 14th and 17th Divisions and troops brought in from Kabul. Militia forces would also play a major role in the offensive. The Soviet 70th

Above right: This Mi-17 Hip-H helicopter was 'road-running' at an altitude of five metres in Jadji in June 1987, when it was hit by Afghans with an RPG-7. Low altitude and night flight, along with continued reliance on active infrared jammers (mounted on the dorsal spine), flare dispensers under the tail boom, and the use of shrouding on the engine exhausts have been among the tactical Stinger countermeasures. (Afghan Media Resource Centre, Peshawar)

Motorized Rifle Brigade backed them up, but wanting to minimize their own casualties, the Soviets let the regime carry out the main thrust of the offensive. The Kabul regime sent its Minister of Defence and Minister of Interior to the scene, probably to follow up on the Zhawar and Herat offensives of 1986, to show the Resistance, and the world, that despite the Stingers and increased political infighting in Kabul, the regime's military could fight its own battles and was going to last.

Preceded by the usual massive air and artillery strikes, the offensive began on 22 May, but soon ran into fierce opposition. The Resistance had built many shelters around Arghandab, and the artillery had not disrupted their defences. The relatively few Resistance Stingers in the area soon started to take their toll of Soviet and Kabul regime helicopters, so close air support was soon limited.

The offensive failed to produce the quick, Press-worthy victory Kabul had hoped for. Rather, Kabul regime forces were committed to intense, close-range fighting against well-armed, competent Resistance forces. For the Communist troops, shaky at the best of times, this was too much, especially when it became apparent that the Soviet helicopter gunships they had come to depend on for so much of their firepower were not being committed to the battle. Kabul regime morale started to crack; large numbers of troops refused to attack Resistance positions. According to reliable but unconfirmed sources, 200 were summarily executed. Other units were subjected to air and artillery bombardment, either accidentally or after they had started to switch sides. More than 1,200 Kabul regime troops went over to the Resistance, many with their arms.

The militia suffered as well. Ismatullah ended up feuding with Kabul, a process that included a gun battle at the December Party Conference. The Baluch morale was shaken. Only the Jowzjan militia – which might be directly in Soviet pay rather than fighting for Kabul – fought hard. By the end of June, the offensive had fizzled out. Communist losses included five to sixteen aircraft (different estimates), more than 30 tanks and AFVS, and 500 troops killed and wounded. Resistance losses were much less. Arghandab showed that the Soviet attempt to create an independent Kabul regime operational capability and to use Kabul regime forces to carry out offensive operations backed up by Soviet airpower, as shown in 1986 at Zhawar and Herat, was not going to work in 1987. Soviet airpower, faced with Stingers, could no longer make it too costly for the Resistance to fight it out with Kabul regime forces, who were now cracking under the pressure of the fighting.

The Battle of Arghandab demonstrated that Resistance forces could fight together effectively even when they were from many different parties and were not dominated by any single leader, and the result was crumbling Kabul regime morale, marked by large-scale combat refusals and desertions.

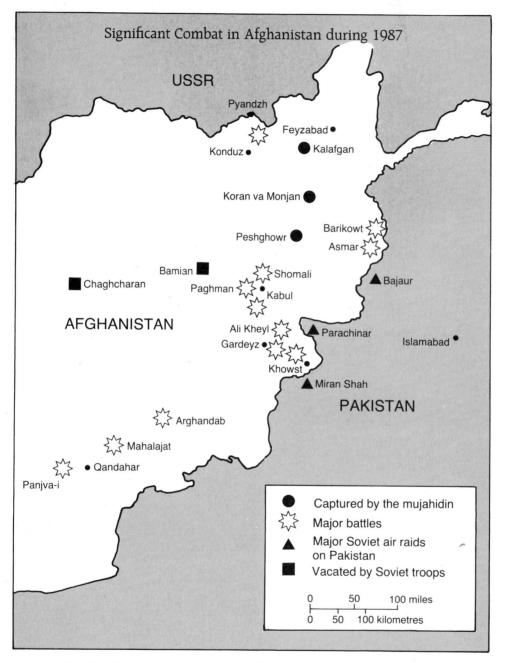

Significant Combat in Afghanistan during 1987

●	Captured by the mujahidin
☆	Major battles
▲	Major Soviet air raids on Pakistan
■	Vacated by Soviet troops

to-air missiles, heralding a significant change in the way the war was fought. By the end of the year, aircraft losses were mounting quickly.

1987

In 1987, the Soviets looked more to political rather than military forces to fight the war. Najibullah declared a unilateral ceasefire to promote National Reconciliation, but neither the idea nor the tactic received much acceptance outside the defensive perimeters of Kabul, Jalalabad, Mazar-e-Sharif and other secure areas. The Soviets soon found that dealing with Najibullah had many of the same frustrations as dealing with Karmal and he was recalled to the Soviet Union for consultations in the summer of 1987. Following another Com-

Above: The weapon and the men that changed the course of the war on the battlefield in 1986–7: the General Dynamics Stinger heat-seeking SAM held for the camera by a trained Resistance gunner. Despite Press criticism that Stingers were too complex for US soldiers, let alone *mujahideen*, the Afghans have shown an ability to deal with sophisticated weapons. The British Army discovered the same with Victorian-era high-technology – repeating rifles and breech-loading cannon – to its cost at the battle of Maiwand.

munist version of the *Loya Jirga* in November, which underlined rather than glossed over the many divisions in the regime, Najibullah presided over the adoption of a new constitution in December 1987.

The constitution bore Najibullah's stamp. Whether the Russians approved of all or part was uncertain. It changed the regime's name to simply the Republic of Afghanistan, dropping the 'democratic' tag that many decidedly non-democratic regimes feel the need of in their title. Non-Communist political parties were to be permitted, and two were established, albeit by long-standing participants in 'National Reconciliation'. Local and parliamentary elections were ostentatiously held (also in April 1988) with the expected pro-regime results. Substantively, Najibullah ruled out anything other than cosmetic power-sharing and retained a monopoly of power for the PDPA.

The political tactics were paralleled by diplomatic ones. Kabul regime officials went on a world-wide diplomatic tour, which did not stop the UN General Assembly vote against the Soviet war being higher than ever, with 124 nations in favour. Part of Soviet political strategy in 1987–8 was an attempt to influence the policies of Pakistan and Iran. Iran, though anxious for Soviet support in its war with Iraq, was wary of Soviet overtures. Soviet pressure on Pakistan was increased mainly with the aim of cutting aid to the Resistance. In addition to offers of a multi-billion dollar aid package, there were continued cross-border attacks by Communist aircraft. Pakistani F-16s claimed one Fitter and one 'own goal' F-16. But in 1987, throughout Pakistan, the Soviets mounted a substantial campaign of state-supported terrorism; using the WAD (KHAD promoted to a full Ministry of State Security) as their executive agent, the KGB ran a campaign of bombings throughout Pakistan, hoping to increase war-weariness and anti-Afghan sentiment. The Pakistani Government, however, played down the bombings and held firm.

The spring and early summer of 1987 brought the most serious Communist battle-field defeats since 1979, as the Stingers helped transform the war in a way that surprised even the Afghans. An offensive against Arghandab, near Kandahar, by Kabul regime troops in May–June, collapsed after heavy fighting. Afghan pilots rioted at Bagram airbase (a year before, at Shindand airbase, they had destroyed their own MiGs). The Soviet attempt to rebuild the Kabul regime army crumbled in the face of a more powerful Resistance and increased PDPA factionalism. An offensive into the Jadji area of Paktia, failed after stout guerrilla resistance. A Soviet offensive against the Maidan area, west of Kabul, also failed with heavy losses to aircraft caused by Stingers. Following this, the Soviets withdrew many of their more isolated battalion and smaller-sized positions, consolidating them into larger garrisons, leaving exposed positions to the Kabul regime forces. Because these Soviet garrisons had frequently served as 'anvil' to the 'hammer' of Soviet offensives, it was a significant tactical reversal.

Soviet air losses peaked in early summer, then rapidly declined as airpower was driven off the battlefield. Even though only a

JADJI

The 1987 Paktia offensive, had Soviet troops as its cutting edge. These included a high percentage of special operations forces—airborne, air assault, *spetsnaz*—combat veterans, their tactics sharpened by years of combat experience. Committed to the Jadji offensive along with the Soviets were Kabul regime regulars and tribal militia. Like the 1985 offensives into Paktia, it included both the relief of a besieged garrison, Ali Sher in Jadji, as its immediate objective and as a subsequent objective the blocking of the major Resistance routes into Afghanistan and establishment of observation posts on some of the major heights.

The offensive opened on 20 May. During the opening stages the Soviets relieved Ali Sher, but as they tried to advance towards the Pakistani border, they encountered increasing opposition. The Resistance reacted by bringing in forces from throughout the border areas and from the refugee camps in Pakistan, in one of the largest Afghan concentrations of the war. The numbers stretched the Resistance supply system—checkpoints eventually had to be set up to limit the numbers of Afghans coming in to the battle.

Jalluladin Haqani came north from his rebuilt base at Zhawar with many of his *mujahideen* to join in the fighting. Mohammed Anwar, who had been operating for many years in the Jagdalak area of Kabul province, was also in the thick of the action – his *mujahideen* included some skilled SAM gunners. The commanders and fighting men involved read like a Who's Who of the Afghan Resistance, coming from all seven major Peshawar-based parties. Even without the chance for extensive pre-planning, the different parties all worked well together.

There were significant numbers of Stingers and Blowpipes in Paktia. The Soviets had to limit their use of airstrikes, relying instead on massed artillery fire, including the use of 220mm BM-22 multiple rocket-launchers. Helicopters operated at low altitude, trying to get under the Stinger's effective envelope. This forced them down into the fire of heavy machine-guns and even RPG-7s, which resulted in more losses. The Soviet special operations forces were thus limited in their use of helicopters for tactical mobility, and had to fight the Afghans for the high ground on the route of advance. The Resistance laid dense minefields on all the major avenues of approach and covered them with heavy weapons. The most intense fighting was at Bayan Khel.

As a rule, for a light, irregular force such as the Afghan guerrillas to stand and fight against a force like the Soviet Army is somewhere between counterproductive and self-destructive. But this time, knowing that the Soviets would be sensitive to losses and that the SAMs could hold their airpower at bay, the Resistance held firm. Numbers of Kabul regime troops switched sides and, unable to make headway, it was the Soviets who broke – the Resistance is agreed on that – and 24 days after the offensive opened, the Soviets retreated.

KALAFGHAN

Ahmad Shah Massoud's taking of the Kabul regime garrison at Kalafghan in Takhar Province in northern Afghanistan on 14 July 1987 was part of his 1986–8 campaign of consolidation throughout the mountains of northern Afghanistan. Kalafghan blocked the communication routes between two valleys, where he had organized the Resistance, and leading beyond to Pakistan.

The first phase in the Kalafghan attack was reconnaissance, which went on until just before the assault. This included extensive debriefings of Kabul regime deserters from the garrison. The locations of all weapons and minefields were plotted on a sand-table model, which was then used by Massoud for planning. Resistance scout teams with hand-held video cameras brought back updated film.

Meanwhile, the political work for the attack was considered even more important than the military preparations. Massoud wanted to involve the local commander – who was of the

Harakat party rather than Jamiat-i-Islami like Massoud – and therefore extensive political work was required to win over the locals, defeating suspicion that co-operation would bring Soviet retaliation, or that Massoud cared only for the Panjshir Valley and the Panjshiris.

The third stage, the military preparations, lasted fifteen days before the assault. The attackers would include 200 men of Massoud's central forces – about 25 per cent of them Panjshiris – plus 100 of the local forces. The central forces troops were concentrated in a remote assembly area 40km from Kalafghan so as to avoid alerting the defenders. A day before the attack, fifteen trucks picked up the central forces troops and some of the locals and carried them to within a one or two hour march from the line of departure. There they were met by the rest of the local forces and more than 100 donkeys to carry the ammunition and heavy weapons – including many Chinese-made, single barrel 107mm rocket-launchers – forward. This created a security problem, not only with the noise and braying of the donkeys, but the area was cordoned off to prevent civilians seeing the movement forward. The troops spent the day before the attack resting in villages near the line of departure, while the firing positions for the heavy weapons were set up. Massoud himself made a two-hour command reconnaissance and tested his radio net before the attack.

The Kalafghan garrison had received warnings of an attack, both from informers and from Kabul, but they had received no less than 70 attack warnings that year, and thought that, at worst, it would be no more than the usual harassment from the local Resistance. They had no idea that Massoud was in the area and had targeted them.

At 17.00 hours a brief but intense barrage by 107mm rockets from firing positions set up within 1,000m of the perimeter overwhelmed the Kabul regime heavy weapons which managed to fire only three mortar rounds. Moving swiftly through the gaps in the minefield plotted during the reconnaissance phase, central forces troops, followed closely by the local *mujahideen*, were through the perimeter and took all five Communist strongpoints in 45 minutes. Only one Communist officer escaped; the rest of the garrison was killed or captured. Resistance losses were extremely light.

Kalafghan had depended for its defence on final protective firing from a battery of howitzers positioned at a Soviet Army firebase. But Massoud had positioned a battery of mortars within striking range of the firebase. Precisely at 17.00 they fired an intense bombardment, suppressing the Soviet guns which could not answer the frantic radio calls from Kalafghan. Finally getting into action, the Soviets then tried to engage the mortars, but the Resistance gunners, having fired off all their ammunition, had by then left. To reduce still further the chances of support reaching Kalafghan, the road between the Soviet firebase and Kalafghan had been heavily mined before the assault. Massoud positioned an ambush force along the road, waiting for a possible relief column.

As soon as night fell, the Resistance started clearing up the battlefield. Massoud called up 25 trucks he had held in readiness to pull out his forces, the prisoners, and all the captured weapons and supplies before dawn. The last truck to leave saw six Soviet helicopters approach, but they did not attack.

The Soviets did not return to Kalafghan until two or three days later. A mixed force of Soviet and Kabul regime troops assembled at the Soviet firebase. Moving along the road to Kalafghan, they encountered Massoud's landmines and the stay-behind ambush force. Finally, fighting their way through, the Soviets arrived at a totally destroyed and stripped Kalafghan. They did not try and re-establish the post (the Communists have re-established none of the posts taken by Massoud in 1986–8) but headed back to the firebase – and into another ambush. Because, each time, it was the Soviet element of the column that was ambushed, there was much Soviet suspicion that Kabul regime forces had been co-operating with the Resistance.

Meanwhile, the division of the spoils from Kalafghan took place, having been pre-decided to avoid bickering. Massoud made sure all the local groups received some captured weapons, evidence that co-operation does pay off. The local *Hezb-i-Islami* (Hekmatyar) commander, however, had proven unco-operative throughout the campaign and some of the Resistance forces had to be detailed to watch them. Yet in other respects, Kalafghan was an effective coalition battle: Massoud had worked very well with fighting men from different parties. Kalafghan demonstrated that forts can be taken by Resistance forces in a well-planned, determined assault, even with a lack of specialized mine-clearing equipment and training.

few hundred Stingers and a smaller number of Blowpipes were initially supplied, at their peak the Stingers were scoring a 68 per cent kill ratio. Total 1987 air losses were estimated at 150–200. Artillery, especially long-range BM-22 220mm multiple rocket-launchers, were emphasized instead of airstrikes. Fighter-bombers attacked from high altitude with minimal accuracy, or at night. Helicopter countermeasures included dropping flares, carrying infra-red jammers, and shielding jet exhausts against the heat-seeking missiles. Meanwhile, in de-populated border areas, some farmers returned to work their fields under protection of the Stingers.

Ismael Khan moved to emulate Massoud's regional strategy in the west, holding a regional Council in Ghowr Province and establishing a 'Council of the West' to match Massoud's 'Council of the North'. Massoud himself continued his protracted war strategy, but took a number of Kabul regime garrisons at Kalafghan and Koran van Monjon in 1987. Other Resistance offensive operations included Operation 'Avalanche', a large-scale cutting of the Kabul–Jalalabad highway in June, and increased pressure on the border forts, including a co-ordinated series of attacks in the Kunar Valley in October–November and a renewed siege of Khost. In March, there were several cross-border attacks on the Soviet Union although, as in the past, these led to intense reprisal bombings and offensives into Kunduz and Takhar provinces which caused heavy civilian casualties. In addition, the Soviets undertook immediate deportations of their own population in many border areas. April saw an offensive against Resistance bases in Baghlan, but the regime outposts put into the area were largely taken a month later by a Resistance counter-attack.

Increased pressure on Khost – because of Stingers, air resupply had become perilous – required a large Soviet offensive to relieve the garrison in the last days of 1987 and the first days of 1988.

1988

Diplomacy again overshadowed the battlefield as new emphasis was put on the Geneva negotiating process. The Soviet foreign minister's announcement of the desire for a withdrawal within a year was made in January, followed by the well-publicized Soviet announcement, in February, that if an agreement were reached by 15 March the withdrawal would begin 60 days after that, electrified the participants,

Above: In 1987, while the Resistance repeatedly attacked Soviet outposts along the Salang Pass Highway, this convoy and many others continued to roll into Kabul. But the southern route, Herat–Kandahar–Kabul, was often cut during 1987. The difficulty of convoy movement in Afghanistan is shown by the fact that the Soviets allow truck drivers to paint a white star on their cab for each successful round-trip, and few trucks show more than about fifteen of them.

grown cynical over the six years of talks. Pakistan, fearful of a continuing war that would block the return of refugees, held firm to the demand for a transition government to take over from the Kabul regime until practically the last moment before withdrawing it under pressure from Washington and also in recognition of the difficulties the Resistance had in organizing themselves. The Pakistanis also made concessions with regard to the timetable of the withdrawal. A meeting between Gorbachev and Najibullah in Tashkent on 7 April put the seal on Moscow's efforts to deliver Kabul regime compliance with their policies.

The terror campaign in Pakistan con-tinued, although the explosion in an ammunition dump near Rawalpindi on 10 April that destroyed much of the results of a pre-agreement supply surge may have been an accident.

The Resistance, pressured by the fast pace of diplomatic events, followed with the creation of a Peshawar-based 'interim government' in February, with Ahmad Shah, Sayeff's number two, as nominal chief. Answering the Kabul regime's attempted outreach to the Resistance and its supporters in the 1987 constitution, the new government left seats open for those aligned with the Kabul regime – especially non-PDPA and army members – who might wish to join,

---

THE GENEVA ACCORDS

The UN-sponsored indirect talks between Pakistan and the Kabul regime (in a war between the Afghan Resistance and the Soviet Union, neither were parties, although the Soviets were part of the regime's delegation and the Pakistanis kept the Resistance leadership informed) started in June 1982. The talks were 'indirect' because the Pakistanis refused to recognize the Kabul regime and so would not sit at the same table. Iran, though invited, would not participate without Resistance representation. Throughout the process, the Special Representative of the Secretary General, Diego Cordovez, shuttled between delegations in Geneva, or, when there was no session there, between capitals.

Pre-Gorbachev, there was little movement, but in December 1985 the Communists first discussed a timetable for a Soviet withdrawal. At first they presented an impossibly long time-frame, but Gorbachev's statement to the Party Congress in February 1986 of a withdrawal 'in the near future' gave the first, faint cause for optimism. Nothing more came of the Geneva process until the failure of 'National Reconciliation' and the unilateral ceasefire called in January 1987, by the Kabul regime, matched with the battlefield reverses of Communist forces. An intense diplomatic push in early 1988 yielded the final agreement. The document finally signed on 14 April 1988 provided:

> Mutual 'non-interference and non-intervention' between Pakistan and Afghanistan (which mandated a cuff-off in the supply of arms for the Resistance without mandating a cut-off in Soviet support for the Kabul regime).
> Encouragement of voluntary return of Afghan refugees.
> Withdrawal of all Soviet troops within nine months.
> The USSR and USA to guarantee the terms.

The Resistance had no standing in the agreement and were mentioned only as 'mercenaries' whom Pakistan agreed not to support. Because the asymmetry of the terms had proven unacceptable to the US Congress, there was a private 'understanding' between the Soviets and Americans that if the Soviet Union kept supporting the Kabul regime, the USA would continue to supply arms to the Resistance. Despite this, there was considerable opposition to the accords not only, understandably, from the Resistance but also from some members of Congress. Senator Gordon Humphrey called it a 'slow-motion sell-out' and pointed out that continued US aid to the Resistance, while permitted under the separate US–Soviet agreement, would violate the main agreements. The Soviets stated that the 60-day delay in implementation was to give the Pakistanis time to dismantle Resistance facilities in their country. The Kabul regime also reserved the right to retain Soviet 'advisers' (numbers unspecified) under the provisions of the 1921 treaty.

while provincial councils would provide decentralized government. This flowed from Pakistan's January 1988 acceptance that former Kabul regime members could participate in a successor government; Khalis, elected as leader for two years the previous October, resigned and was replaced first by Hekmatyar and, in June 1988, by Gailani, returning to the old three-month rotation.

On the battlefield, the impact of the relief of Khost lasted but a few weeks. In March, another offensive was launched that relieved the fort at Urgun, also in Paktia province. In the north, Ahmad Shah Massoud continued to assault regime outposts, taking Burqua in January, and started moving down the Panjshir in April, taking regime garrisons. Before the Soviet withdrawal started, more reinforcements arrived to cover it and, in April, a mechanized column pushed down the main road from Kandahar to Ghazni to keep it open.

Barikot was abandoned on 22 April, followed by other posts in the upper Kunar and in Paktia (Ali Khel, Chowni, and Chamkani). In April–June, the siege of Khost resumed after two transport aircraft fell to Stingers in March, again cutting off daylight airlifts. In the south, garrisons were pulled back towards Kandahar. As early as March, the Kandahar Resistance had gone over to the offensive, taking the district capital at Panjuai, west of Kandahar, on the main road

to Herat; Darwazgui, Athgul in Zabul province and Maruf, near Kandahar, all fell within days. The Soviets left Qalat, the provincial capital of Zabul on 18 April, but Kabul regime troops held out until 18 June, when it became the first provincial capital to be entered by the Resistance since 1979. In the west, the Soviets pulled their troops towards the airfields at Herat and Shindand, the regime garrison at Khak-e-Safid near Shindand falling on 4 April. In May, the first major Soviet unit (starting, as promised, on the 15th), the 66th Motorized Rifle Brigade, left Jalalabad for the Soviet border. While it encountered only light resistance, other Soviet troop movements have not been as fortunate. In mid-June, the Resistance even succeeded in blocking the road between Ghazni and Kabul, forcing the withdrawing forces at Ghazni to take a longer route. But, on the whole, the Afghans have not been trying to destroy departing Soviets.

Najibullah, taunting that 'Nobody has taken Kabul in the past and nobody will take it in the future,' was not giving up without fighting, not only on the battlefield but politically and diplomatically. He brought non-PDPA members into the government, and made diplomatic overtures to India (warmly received) and the West (rebuffed). Other changes were seen in the north, suggesting that that might be his 'national redoubt'. The Kabul defences were indeed

KHOST, 1987–8

In late 1987, the Kabul regime garrison at Khost, which had been supplied primarily by air, was under attack by Resistance forces. Unlike the attempt to take Khost in the summer of 1985, this time the Resistance could use the Stingers to reduce the effect of Soviet airpower. In October, resupply flights had to be halted. While Khost was not in imminent danger of falling, the situation was apparently serious enough for the Soviets to put together a force of 20,000 troops and commit them to fighting their way through to Khost. These forces were predominantly Russian: multiple regiment forces from both 103rd Guards Airborne Division and 108th Motorized Rifle Division, its tank battalions equipped with T-72 main battle tanks, large numbers of non-divisional engineers and artillery, helicopters, and a special operations brigade. Two squadrons of Su-25 Frogfoot fighter-bombers deployed to Bagram airfield from the Soviet Union to lend support while the Kabul regime's 7th, 8th and 12th Divisions also contributed columns. The immediate objective was to break through the mountains between Gardez and Khost, the ultimate goal being the relief of Khost.

After extensive reconnaissance, the Soviets decided that the shortest and most direct route to Khost would be the best, and, starting on 1 November, troops began to concentrate around Gardez. The Resistance, well aware of what was going on, brought in reinforcements. Jalulladin Haqani boasted that the Soviets would, as in 1985, fail to get through.

Jumping off at the end of November, two divisions and one brigade of Soviet airborne troops moved forward towards the Sadan Kamvan and Sato Kandau Passes through which runs the main Gardez–Khost road. The Kabul regime divisions were in the first echelon, with the Soviets in overwatch positions, one attacking on each side of the road. They soon encountered heavy resistance, with large-scale use of 107mm rockets. The Soviets responded with massed artillery fire, especially 152mm howitzers, firing 'beehive' rounds at close range, each containing thousands of deadly dart-like flechettes. The long-ranged BM-22 220mm multiple rockets pounded Resistance positions through the depth of the mountains and fighter-bombers attacked from high altitude.

But the Soviets were not relying on firepower alone, but also added some original manoeuvres to their operation. A brigade-sized force of Kabul regime forces, starting from Urgun, made an enveloping march through the mountains, guided by local militia. This threatened to cut off the Resistance forces at the north ends of the passes, who withdrew.

The Soviets, their initial objective within sight, in a surprise move, flew in an airborne brigade by helicopters, at night, to seize Mirujan at the south end of the mountains along the Gardez–Khost road. The helicopters came in low, trying to stay under the Stingers' effective altitude; the ploy was an effective use of vertical envelopment.

Meanwhile, in another night airlift, a Soviet airborne brigade was flown into Khost and launched a breakout attack northwards towards Gardez.

The Resistance, after the intense fighting at the north ends of the mountains, realized that trying to block the Soviet forces would only lead to casualties being suffered without a purpose. They thoroughly mined the Gardez–Khost road and withdrew away from the road, but kept within 107mm rocket range, forcing the Soviets slowly to move forward to clear the mines under long-range fire. Haqani, as in the 1986 Zhawar fighting, was wounded in action.

As the Soviets' advance continued through December, other heliborne forces were used in their standard role of 'cresting the heights', holding the high ground which the column must pass. Soviet heliborne forces suffered losses to the heavily armed Resistance when they went too far forward; there were no survivors from one platoon of 44 troopers inserted unawares into a waiting Resistance ambush. Towards the end of December, however, the column pushing south from Gardez linked up with that pushing north from Khost. The first Soviet armoured spearheads entered Khost on 30 December and more followed during the next few days. Soviet and regime outposts were kept along the Khost–Gardez road for much of January, then withdrawn,

The Khost fighting was, overall, less intense than either the 1985, 1986 or 1987 Paktia offensives, although losses were not light. Total Resistance fatalities were probably about 150–300, those of the Communists at least twice that. Unlike previous Soviet offensives, this one received extensive Press coverage in Moscow while in progress and the well-publicized Khost fighting may have been intended to allow the Soviet Army to go out on a victory. Khost may have been an attempt to reverse the lessons of the Jadji fighting of 1987, to show that the Soviet Army can still go wherever it wants to go in Afghanistan.

Right: By 1988, over 1,000 Communist aircraft had been lost as a result of the war in Afghanistan. This was an Mi-8 Hip-C helicopter. Probably about half of the helicopters lost were as a result of operational accidents. But Afghanistan has given the Soviets a cadre of battle-tested helicopter operators and planners, though the events of 1986–8 showed them that just a few Stingers can greatly increase the cost of using them. (Committee for a Free Afghanistan)

formidable, but vulnerable to interdiction.

The first provincial capitals taken in June were later abandoned in the face of superior firepower, as was the city of Kunduz, first handed over to the Resistance and then abandoned by them after a counterattack preceded by heavy air attacks in August and September. This led to the Resistance suspending large-scale attacks on cities, although by October seven provincial capitals had been abandoned to them. Throughout the summer, the Soviet withdrawal continued, reaching the half-way point in August, by which time even Soviet generals were publicly stating that the Kabul regime was unlikely to long survive the Soviet withdrawal in its present form. The Panjshir and, by October, the Kunar valleys were abandoned to the Resistance.

In August, President Zia of Pakistan, the most significant foreign supporter of the Resistance, was killed in a plane crash along with the US ambassador and most of the Pakistani high command. The cause – sabotage by Pakistani radicals or WAD was suspected – remained uncertain. The death of Zia, however, came too late to affect Pakistani support for the Resistance in 1988, but it meant that Hekmatyar would no longer receive backing as a chosen instrument of political power.

The Communist hold deteriorated most rapidly in the south. The approaches to Kandahar were cleared by calling in Noorzai tribe to defeat their traditional rivals the Ackakzai, who fought for Kabul. By October, after Spin Boldak on the Pakistani border fell, Kabul troops were pressed back to the gates of Kandahar as the Soviets withdrew.

In Kabul, to reduce the danger of a Khalq coup, their leadership was sent abroad or eased away from power. Army leadership was reshuffled. Najibullah was expected to be dropped from the payroll, but no obvious successor was likely to fare better. A new high-calibre Soviet ambassador, Yuli Vorontsov, was sent to Kabul in order to help reach a political solution where General Zaitsev had failed in achieving a military one.

While the Resistance remained politically divided, the fighting men proved resistant to suggestions of a coalition including PDPA members. Trips inside Afghanistan by Khalis, Hekmatyar, Rabbani, Gailani and Mojadidi were evidence that The power has shifted more to field commanders and, secondarily, to tribal leadership. The continued importance of tribal links shows that traditional Afghanistan ways of conflict resolution still work, evidence that Afghanistan is unlikely to become Lebanon. Meanwhile, in Peshawar, there were frantic attempts to put together a political presence for 1989, while the UN started to look at the tremendous task of reconstruction.

The Resistance did not try and destroy withdrawing Soviet forces or mount pitched assaults on cities, preparing to wait until the Soviet withdrawal finished, although barrages of 122mm Egyptian-made rockets continued. These destroyed a massive munitions dump at Kalgay in August. In response, terrorist incidents in Pakistan continued and cross-border air attacks increased, with the Pakistanis shooting down several intruders.

In early November, the Soviets escalated, while appealing to the UN to help bring about a coalition that would be acceptable to Moscow. The withdrawal was halted; 30 MiG-27 Flogger-D fighter-bombers and batteries of SS-1 Scud-B surface-to-surface missiles arrived in Afghanistan and were used in combat, as were Tu-26 Backfire strategic bombers flying from the Soviet Union. Kabul regime forces counterattacked eastwards from Jalalabad. Ahmad Shah Massoud, who had been using his central forces as the cadre for a 13,000-man army intended to liberate seven provinces and, if needed, cut off Kabul after the Soviet withdrawal, moved to interdict the Salang Pass in response. It seems that neither these new Soviet weapons, nor the Pakistani general election, had an immediate impact on the overall military situation, although it did raise questions over Soviet intentions to honour the Geneva accords.

3. THE SOVIET WAR IN AFGHANISTAN

Strategy – The International Context

Afghanistan has been a significant – though never crucial – issue in Soviet relations with the rest of the world. But if, as many commentators believe, Gorbachev would like to see Soviet resources shifted to economic development, with access to foreign technology, in a world with western Europe neutralized and decoupled from the United States, which, in turn, would be largely impotent on the world scene, it would be a good idea to remove Afghanistan as an issue.

Soviet strategic aims have remained relatively constant throughout the war in Afghanistan. The invasion and subsequent involvement has demonstrated that the Soviets can and will use military force to alter political situations on their periphery, and it is uncertain whether this will change under Gorbachev. The apparent intention is to maintain a government in Kabul acceptable to Moscow, a goal that was furthered by Soviet military, political, and diplomatic actions in 1980–8. Whether any government in Kabul acceptable to Moscow will prove, in the future, also to be acceptable to the Afghan people and so lead to the return of the refugee populations from Pakistan and Iran is unlikely. Yet, as late as November 1988, such a government remained the Soviet goal.

The Soviet policy towards Afghanistan, both internally and in the international context, has also been oriented towards demonstrating the Soviet view that internal counter-revolution is unacceptable, another element that appears unlikely to change under Gorbachev. Backing this up is the whole range of what the Soviets call 'active measures' to influence the situation, both inside Afghanistan and in the world, this being backed up by disinformation, propaganda, psychological operations, and intelligence and covert activities. This approach, in place throughout most of the war with limited success, had obviously run foul of reality by 1988.

Gorbachev would consider a broader range of successor governments more acceptable than Brezhnev would have done, and the Soviets obviously do not want a Moscow-approved government to fall to Islamic guerrillas. This would certainly be a bad precedent for their own Islamic population – in 1988 by no means a powder keg of unrest, but apparently dissatisfied with the war – and Marxist states world-wide.

The Soviet war is certainly not popular with the world community, as the increasing UN General Assembly votes calling for withdrawal of all foreign troops show. Nor is the war just one of the wide range of issues dividing the West and the Soviet Union. The repeated votes in the UN General Assembly, the Organization of the Islamic Conference, and other international bodies reveal a broad and impressive consensus of international opinion opposing the Soviet war in Afghanistan. A consensus on action is harder to achieve. Perhaps the better gauge of Afghanistan's world context is seen not in the General Assembly votes, but in the absence of Security Council action or the absence of effective action by the Non-Aligned Movement.

The outcome of low-intensity conflicts is often determined by external factors. Whether the Soviets have won in Afghanistan will in large part be determined not by whether Soviet or PDPA regime soldiers remain in Kabul, but only when it is seen how Soviet interests are served by developments (including the nature of the post-1990 successor governments) in the two regions Afghanistan borders: Iran and the Gulf, Pakistan and the sub-continent. As far back as Lenin's time, Moscow has believed that the broad masses of these areas, led by Leninist vanguard parties and motivated and protected by the Soviet Union, can give

them key leverage against the west. On 5 August 1919, Leon Trotsky told the Central Committee of the Soviet Communist Party: 'The road to Paris and London lies through the towns of Afghanistan, the Punjab and Bengal.' Then, as now, a presence in Afghanistan has had the potential of increasing geopolitical leverage against Iran (Russia has invaded or occupied Persian territory on eleven occasions since the eighteenth century) and the Gulf, both areas of long-standing Soviet concern. Foreign Minister

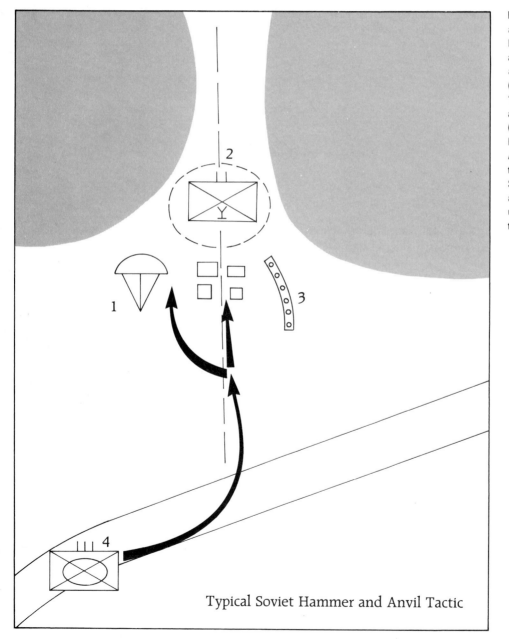

Left: Soviet 'hammer and anvil' cordon tactics. Following preliminary air and artillery strikes (1), an air assault battalion (2) is lifted in to form a 'stop group' behind the area to be swept. Mines (3) are dropped from helicopters to prevent Afghans slipping through the cordon. A mixed Soviet-DRA combined arms force (4) slowly moves up the road to sweep through each village.

Typical Soviet Hammer and Anvil Tactic

V. M. Molotov, on 26 November 1940, wrote: 'The area south of Batum and Baku in the general direction of the Persian Gulf is ... the centre of aspirations of the Soviet Union'. But, by 1987–8, it must have been questionable in Moscow whether the war was furthering or harming whatever aspirations still existed.

The expansion of the airfields at Shindand and Kandahar in the south of Afghanistan in 1980–2 added a significant military component to Soviet regional and geopolitical leverage during the course of the war. Soviet relations with India have improved throughout the course of the war in Afghanistan while expansion of Soviet relations with the Gulf states is as much because of Afghanistan as in spite of it. Also, due in part to the Iran-Iraq war, the Soviets are now a force to be considered in both the sub-continent and the Gulf.

Strategy – The Struggle in Afghanistan, 1978–88

The strategy, like the tactics, of Soviet low-intensity conflict is by no means purely, or even primarily, military. Afghanistan has illustrated that. To the Soviets, a complex situation such as Afghanistan had to be basically a political event, with the role of military action being to make political consolidation possible.

While ideally, the Soviets will try and create or, preferably, co-opt indigenous leaders and groups, including the use of 'national fronts' with 'non-party' figures which facilitated the Soviet consolidation of power in much of eastern Europe, the 'National Fatherland Front' in Afghanistan and the more recent 'National Reconciliation' policy have had little success simply because the Kabul regime's legitimacy and credibility has been extremely low throughout the 1978–88 period. The overall situation that led to the Communist assumption of power in pre-war Mongolia or post-war eastern Europe (especially a victorious Red

Army either in-place or on the borders) simply could not be re-created in Afghanistan.

Since the 1979 invasion, the Soviets have had their PDPA surrogates turn away from supporting the brutal and hamfisted attempts at radical social reform which characterized their rule in 1978–9. Utilizing the existing institutions – especially Islam – has had priority instead of trying swiftly and violently to restructure society. By 1980, the Soviets had obviously decided, in Afghanistan, that the in-place social, cultural and religious structures were the strongest. Islam was used as much as possible to legitimize Kabul regime rule in Afghanistan, just as 'Red Mullahs' were used in Central Asia in the 1920s–1930s. They have apparently put more emphasis on this than building Communist institutions. True, the PDPA managed to expand to 70,000 actual (185,000 claimed) members, but many of those that have supported it have been opportunists or driven to support the regime by non-ideological reasons, most often being tribal or religious differences with the Resistance. The only major success of a purely PDPA-organized institution was the WAD, which was in large part made possible by large-scale KGB assistance.

Traditional divide-and-conquer tactics, exploiting linguistic, ethnic, tribal or religious divisions, had little success in Afghanistan during 1978–88, despite the lack of a centralized resistance. Mainly due to the pervading, shared impact of Islam, no major resistance leader or group has changed sides, rather, only a limited number of local commanders, usually with a few hundred men apiece, have come over to the PDPA.

The Soviets and the Kabul regime have had more success in bribing Resistance commanders to refrain from attacking specific locations or in arranging local truces. Kabul regime commanders (or in the case of Ahmad Shah Massoud in 1983–4, the Soviets themselves) often arrange ceasefires with Resistance commanders. It is likely that many local agreements have already been made between the Resistance and the different elements of the Kabul regime armed forces and government about what to do if the Soviets do finally withdraw.

Command and Control

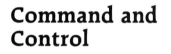

The standard hierarchy of national and military decision-making is frequently inappropriate during counter-insurgency conflicts. Relatively low-level activities, both political and military, can be of high-level interest. Soviet military operations and tactics operated under centralized top-down command. The initial invasion saw the use of the High Command of the Southern Theatre of Strategic Military Action (TVD) under the direct command of the then Assistant Minister of Defence Sokolov, dispatched from Moscow to run the invasion directly. The High Command of the Southern TVD (since 1985 under General Mikhail M. Zaitsev, former Commander Group Soviet Forces Germany) has, reportedly, authority over the overall conflict. The Turkestan Military District in the Soviet Union handled much of the mobilization before the 1979 invasion and, afterwards, logistics and service support for the troops inside Afghanistan.

The Soviet armed forces outside the Ministry of Defence – the MVD Internal Security Troops and the KGB Border Troops – have also been involved in the war in Afghanistan. The MVD was probably involved in the initial invasion – especially their own *spetsnaz* forces – and since then have handled security on the Soviet side of the border as well as providing advisers to the Kabul regime. The KGB Border Troops have had a more active role, providing advisers to Kabul regime Border Troops and being in action against Resistance raids over the Soviet border and operating in North Afghanistan since the early 1980s. Two battalion-sized forces operated on the main routes from the Soviet Union, ranging as far south as Herat and Kabul.

The Limited Contingent of Soviet Forces in Afghanistan (LCSFA), a title reviled in the 9 May 1988 *Izvestia* as 'that armchair general's bureaucratic term', included, in 1980–8, the Headquarters of the Soviet 40th Army, subordinate to the LCSFA. 40th Army acted as its operational command structure, alongside a command structure for air assets. The combat divisions and separate brigades in Afghanistan report to LCSFA, either directly or through 40th Army. It is uncertain to which headquarters the divisions based in the Soviet Union but committed to the war are subordinate.

The operational division of responsibility, however, is different. While separate Soviet and Kabul regime chains of command are

Above left: Kabul regime Air and Air Defence Force trainees with their MiG-21 Fishbed-C, a standard Kabul regime fighter-bomber. These were used extensively in the armed recon-naissance role and to carry out airstrikes throughout Afghanistan, even though they were not suited for these missions. In 1986, a squadron of Fishbeds was destroyed when their aircrew planted explosive charges in them, and then headed for the hills.

Above: A KGB Border Troops cavalry patrol. Such units still patrol the Soviet-Afghan border and have been in action against cross-border Resistance raids. In one action, mounted *mujahideen* under Sayid Mukhtar, a former Afghan Army paratrooper and NIFA Resistance commander from Takhar province, raided a Soviet night position and ran off their horses.

maintained, operationally and tactically there emerged one single command structure, controlled by the Soviets. There has, however, never been a Soviet 'viceroy' in Afghanistan as such, combining military and political command.

Since 1979, the Soviets have aimed to achieve control of the Kabul regime armed forces. As well as state-to-state and party-to-party ties, the Soviets have armed forces-to-armed forces and secret police-to-secret police ties. The Kabul regime command structure, much as it was prior to 1978, has remained in place throughout the war. But soon after the 1979 invasion, the actual authority shifted to Soviet advisers at all levels.

The nominal Kabul regime chain of command runs from the Ministry of Defence in Kabul, to the three geographical corps headquarters and a number of independent divisions and brigades. Under the corps are division headquarters. When more than local operations are required, different regiments and divisions will each contribute a column to a larger force. In 1986–7, a nominally Kabul regime General Staff provided operational command for multi-division operations. Apparently, however, they never had operational control over Soviet units.

Operational control of both Soviet and Kabul regime units was rather, exercised, at least in 1982–8, by two Soviet operational commands (*operativnaya gruppa*) with headquarters at Kabul and Termez in the USSR and a number (seven to eighteen have been reported, possibly at different times) of territorial tactical commands. Throughout the war, rapid operational or tactical response has been limited by the command system, especially in 1980–3. All but urgent calls for airstrikes had to go through Kabul, leading to at least a one-day delay in reacting to targeting information. Troop movements were even longer in response and all were well advertised in advance. From 1984, however, the Soviets have shown a great deal more capability, at a tactical level at least, and special operations forces in particular have proved that they can effectively react to developing situations.

Major offensives have been marked by the dispatch of General Staff representatives from Moscow, who set up forward ground and air-based command posts, with separate dedicated communications links with Moscow. The General Staff in Moscow has also had direct input on the war, possibly, in recent years, by-passing TVD level and using a Lolos satellite com-munications terminal in Kabul to pass direct orders. Command control in offensives have included the provision of airborne command posts.

Military Operations, 1978–88

Throughout their battlefield involvement in Afghanistan, the Soviets have stressed a relatively low level of troop commitment and rate of casualties (apparently more important than the ultimate figure), consistent with the attainment of a long-term solution that emphasized the political rather than the military aspect of the war. This reduced the options for large-scale escalation. There were no repeated systematic offensives by paratroopers, unlike the French in Algeria; limited cross-border airstrikes, unlike Israel or South Africa; and the Soviets have never been able fully to control the Kabul regime. But to the Soviets,

UNIT ORGANIZATION

While Soviet formations, units and sub-units in Afghanistan follow their basic standard organization, there has been a great deal of adaptation to Afghan conditions.

Most forces put into the field are composites. Especially in 1981–3, each Soviet regiment would field one combined arms battalion, consisting of a battalion-sized force of motorized rifle and tank sub-units with most of the regiment's combat support assets. This would leave one-third of the regiment free for training and one-third for local defence and non-combat missions. Soviet organizational innovations in Afghanistan included combined arms (tank and motorized rifle battalions, composite (tube and MRL) artillery battalions and specialized reconnaissance platoons and companies.

The same applies on the defence. Most Soviet units in Afghanistan were not necessarily clustered around their formation headquarters. Until 1987, there were numerous company-, battalion- and regiment-sized garrisons throughout Afghanistan. In 1987, many of these were pulled back, but key ones, such as those along the Salang Pass highway, remained even after the 66th Motorized Rifle Brigade pulled out of Jalalabad, and other Soviet garrisons were concentrated on Kabul, the airfields and the north in 1988.

Right: The most feared and hated fighter-bomber in Afghanistan is the Su-25 Frogfoot. Twelve of them went to Afghanistan in 1981 with the 200th Guards Independent Attack Squadron, being based first at Bagram but then shifting to Shindand. For several years it was the only Frogfoot squadron in the Soviet Air Force. A second squadron was in action from Bagram by early 1986. (US Department of Defense)

Left: A headquarters van near Kabul, part of the considerable Soviet command, control, communications and intelligence infrastructure in place.

Right: The most significant weapon in the war: an Mi-24 Hind-D. Since the 1970s, the Soviets have invested many billions of dollars in their helicopter force. That a few Stinger SAMs could reduce the effectiveness of the helicopters and the absence of reliable anti-Stinger counter-measures must have raised questions about the validity of Soviet helicopters in a European conflict. (US Department of Defense)

Right: These Mi-17 Hip-Hs at Jalalabad airfield about 1985–6 have no revetments or hangarettes, despite repeated Resistance attacks on the airfield, including one, in January 1983, which led to the destruction of a squadron of helicopters. (National Islamic Front of Afghanistan)

low intensity does not mean low technology. Many of the weapons used in Afghanistan have been among the most modern in the Soviet arsenal. On the battlefield, since 1980, the Soviets have tried to make maximum use of firepower, whether from Soviet or Kabul regime bombers, fighter-bombers, attack helicopters, long-range tube and rocket artillery (increasingly important after the introduction of the Stinger), and even surface-to-surface missiles.

Militarily, throughout the course of the war, the Soviets have tried to interdict the increased flow of supplies to the interior (this only became significant when the supply flow was important enough to interdict, starting about 1984). The Soviets have used large-scale bombing to destroy rural agriculture since 1980. Starting in 1982, they improved their intelligence network of aircraft, patrols, sensors, agents, and informers while still looking for a way effectively to apply divide-and-conquer tactics, although this last element had but limited success.

About 80–85 per cent of the Afghan countryside remained outside Communist control even at the height of the Soviet military involvement. The Soviets have tried to exert control in the countryside without occupying it. To do this they have de-populated large areas of countryside, near the roads, in food-producing areas, or along infiltration routes. Mao Tse-Tung wrote, 'The guerrilla must move amongst the people as a fish swims in the sea.' The Soviets were not trying to catch the fish one at a time, but rather draining the ocean. In his 1864 campaign in Virginia's Shenandoah Valley, US General Philip Sheridan gave orders for destruction so thorough that, 'a crow flying over this valley will have to carry his own rations'. The Soviets aimed at and achieved the same level of destruction in many areas of Afghanistan, especially in those areas near the Pakistani and Iranian borders and around Kabul. Other areas, especially in the Turkic-speaking north, were spared. De-population not only removed a rural population that would support the guerrilla, but forced them to Pakistan (to pressure that country) or the Afghan cities (where they can be better watched). The policy also forced the Resistance to carry their own provisions; removed villages that could be used as staging-points for attacks; increased the effectiveness of special operations, removing villagers who could give warning; and helped create areas where any movement seen by aircraft or sensors indicated the Resistance.

The civil population has been the target of most of the massive Soviet firepower: 600,000 dead according to a 1986 voluntary aid group study: 875,000 in a USAID study estimate in 1987; 1,200,000 in a study by the Gallup organization in 1987. As Lenin wrote: 'We have never rejected terror on principle, nor can we do so. Terror is a form of military operation that may be usefully applied.' It certainly has been applied in Afghanistan in 1978–88.

The war has been intensive in some areas, absent in others. Before 1984, in much of Afghanistan, a visitor would not have been aware that a war was going on; the Afghans running things the way they always have. In remote, mountainous areas, such as the Hazara Jat and Nuristan, there has been no attempt to re-impose Communist control since Kabul regime forces were driven out in 1979–80. Instead, these areas have been subjected to Soviet and Kabul regime attempts to divide the local Afghans against one another.

The desire to minimize overall economic cost was reflected by Soviet operations from 1980–8. Afghan natural gas, available in economically significant amounts, was piped across the border as an offset to the 'fraternal assistance'. In 1981–2 the US Defense Intelligence Agency estimated the war effort's cost at one to two per cent of Soviet defence spending. By 1988, the annual figure was estimated in the four to eight billion dollar range; the total cost exceeding fifty billion dollars (this is in market-rate conversion from rouble cost, although estimation of Soviet expenditures is a frequently inexact procedure).

Tactics

Soviet tactics, still (1987–88) largely based on the conventional warfare model, have led to low efficiency in counter-insurgency warfare. Yet the fact remains that the war in Afghanistan has been, in execution if not in result, consistent with the historical experience of Soviet counter-insurgency. On the battlefield, politically and diplomatically, Soviet strategy, operations and tactics during the 1980–8 period have been coherent, complementary and interlocking. This certainly does not support the view of an inept force waging an ineffectual war. Rather, it is an indication that the Soviets see victory as the end of war in low-intensity conflicts as well as those of broader scope, even if this victory cannot be totally realized on the battlefield. The withdrawal starting in May 1988 may not, in fact, be a turning away from the goal of victory, but more likely a desire to pursue it more effectively in Geneva, Islamabad and Washington than among the unforgiving mountains.

Throughout most of the war, about 80 per cent of the Soviet ground forces have been 'conventionally' organized, equipped and trained for service support or combat in

Above: Soviet para-troopers in formation, wearing their prized 'blue berets'. They wear the camouflage overalls that became standard Soviet battledress by mid-war. Paratroops made up the strength not only of the airborne division and independent regiment, but of the air assault brigade and battalion as well. Motorized riflemen who received air assault training were allowed to wear the striped T-shirt as well. (US Department of Defense)

Above right: A Soviet paratrooper fires his AKD 5.45mm folding-stock assault rifle. He is wearing his blue beret for the camera; it would be replaced by a steel helmet or bush hat in combat.

ORDER OF BATTLE; SOVIET ARMY IN AFGHANISTAN, FEBRUARY 1988

HQ, 40th Army	Termez, USSR
40th Army Forward HQ	Kabul, Bala Hisar Fort
103rd Guards Airborne Division	Kabul, South-west Camp
108th Motorized Rifle Division	Kabul, North-east Camp
201st Motorized Rifle Division	Kunduz (withdrew July 1988)
5th Guards Motorized Rifle Division	Shindand
88th Motorized Rifle Division	Kushka, USSR
4th Guards Motorized Rifle Division	Termez, USSR
70th Motorized Rifle Brigade	Kandahar (withdrew September 1988)
66th Motorized Rifle Brigade	Jalalabad (withdrew May 1988)
191st Motorized Rifle Regiment	Ghazni (withdrew June 1988)
866th Motorized Rifle Regiment	Feyzabad
56th Air Assault Brigade	Gardez
375th Guards Airborne Regiment	Bagram
? Spetsnaz Brigade	Shindand
? Spetsnaz Brigade	Kabul
? Airmobile Battalion	Kabul?
40th Artillery Brigade	Kabul
40th Rocket Regiment	Kabul
40th Airfield Defence Battalion	Bagram
KGB Border Troops Mobile Group	Kabul (withdrew 1988)
KGB Border Troops Mobile Group	Herat (withdrew 1988)

mechanized combined-arms operations (the bulk of the motorized rifle and tank forces). The remainder are those special operations forces organized and equipped for actions outside the standard Soviet conventional combined-arms model (including airborne, air assault, *spetsnaz*, KGB Border Troops and specially trained motorized rifle units).

On the battlefield, the Soviets have had great difficulty in adapting an army equipped, organized and trained for mechanized, combined-arms combat in western Europe or Manchuria to fighting a counter-insurgency war. Soviet combined arms mechanized forces, until about 1984, were unable to take advantage of guerrilla inexperience, seldom moved on the high ground, or practised aggressive small-unit tactics. Even after the 1984–6 era of Soviet tactical improvements, the bulk of their forces – motorized rifle units mounted in BTRs or BMPs – remain roadbound with limited tactical flexibility, although they provide the bulk of the Soviet forces for large-scale

Above: A column of up-armoured BMP-1E infantry fighting vehicles, armed with 73mm guns, gets air cover from a two-ship element of Mi-8 Hip-Cs. Most Soviet columns moved with helicopter support; as well as inserting detachments on heights along the route, helicopters would provide reconnaissance (often reconnaissance by fire), suppression, communications relay and casualty evacuation.

ground sweeps and convoy escorts as well as defending key installations.

Soviet combined-arms forces also have extensive logistics requirements. The Afghans soon learned to let armoured columns roll past them and wait for the resupply convoy which would try to come up at the end of the day. The Soviet option of greatly increasing the number of combined arms forces in Afghanistan would also have required them to increase their logistics infrastructure, which in turn would require more troops to supply and guard the infrastructure. This is the same law of diminishing returns that resulted, at the height of the half-million man US commitment to South Vietnam, in only 80,000 troops being in close contact with the enemy. The Soviets have tried to prevent this happening in Afghanistan.

Motorized rifle divisions are not the type of forces that gain victory in counter-insurgency warfare. In the words of Douglas Blaufarb and George Tanham, two veteran US experts in the field, 'the first principle of successful counter-guerrilla tactics is to take the guerrilla as the model and fight him in his own style. . . . This principle means the broad deployment of forces in small units relying largely on weapons they can carry.' Such forces were not part of the Soviet order of battle during the first year of the war, but soon afterwards, they realized they had to develop such a capability within their special operations forces. These had been exten-

sively and effectively used in the 1979 invasion and were re-introduced to combat in about 1981, although their use did not greatly increase until 1984. Soviet special operations forces are trained and equipped for operations either independently – especially in the interdiction mission with ambush patrols deep inside guerrilla territory – or in conjunction with 'standard' combined arms mechanized forces. Operating either heliborne or dismounted, often in forces smaller than those of combined arms columns, they can also achieve an element of surprise, effectively impossible for road-bound mechanized forces, and small teams often used Afghan dress or Kabul regime uniforms for cover. Because they are smaller, they require more precise targeting, hence better intelligence.

Patrolling is the time-tested way of obtaining battlefield intelligence. Even with the increased use of special operations and other heliborne forces during the 1984–6 period, patrolling has been limited in comparison with what Western-style forces have employed in similar counter-insurgency situations. Patrols have been either short- or long-ranged, the latter often inserted by helicopter (sometimes parachute), which led to their being curtailed after the introduction of Stinger SAMs in 1986. Defensive, ambush, reconnaissance and target acquisition patrols are mounted too, supplemented in the last role by Soviet observation posts (OP). Frequently sited on mountain peaks accessible only by helicopter, and surrounded by mines, these OPs are also used to direct air and artillery strikes.

In 1984–7 the Soviets made greater use of heliborne forces capable of extended dismounted operations. The troops of the airborne regiments, the air assault brigade, and one (or more) battalion per motorized rifle division and brigade that have received special training are frequently used for heliborne operations. Helicopters, vital for both firepower and mobility, were still used effectively after the introduction of Stinger and Blowpipe surface-to-air missiles in 1986, but never recovered their tactical pre-eminence.

Failures in mountain warfare by the largely road-bound Soviet Army in 1980–1 led to re-evaluation of their training and the applicability of historical experience in mountain warfare and a crash attempt to obtain Western technology and expertise, buying up large quantites of open-market climbing equipment and books on mountain warfare. As a result, specialized mountain troops appeared in action by 1984. These were probably airborne, special operations forces, or motorized rifle sub-units that had received specialized mountain training. Kabul regime militia have also been used for mountain operations, in their home terrain.

Individual soldier skills and small-unit tactics have been a Soviet weakness, although the Afghans say the Soviets became progressively more adept, especially since early 1984. During the 1979 invasion and early 1980 most of the men of the motorized rifle divisions, as we have seen, were recalled reservists from the Turkestan and Central Asia Military Districts. Often with little refresher training since leaving their conscript service and never mobilized before as part of these divisions, many of these reservists were Muslim, though only a few actually changed sides and joined the Resistance. By mid-1980, the reservists had all

NOTES

In May 1988, before the first Soviet withdrawal, Lieutenant-General Boris Gromov, commander of the LCSFA, reported that his force, 103,000 strong, was positioned at eighteen garrisons and 170 bases inside Afghanistan.

Since 1986, all motorized rifle divisions have had their tank and air defence regiments garrisoned in the Soviet Union.

In 1987, Special Operations Forces (battalion sized) were deployed to Baraki Barak; Chagha Serai, Kunar; and Sirdarabad. In May 1988 they were all withdrawn.

866 MRR has a detachment at Koh-e-Wakhan.

In 1987, the army-level rocket regiment had BM-22 battalions, near Herat, Gardez and in the Kunar Valley (withdrawn May 1988).

In 1987 garrisons at Bamiyan and Chakcharan (battalion strength) were among those withdrawn. Elements of 66th MRB were withdrawn in May 1988.

The number of independent brigades and air assault battalions is uncertain: there is at least one, but motorized rifle divisions and brigades have been reinforced by additional air assault battalions as well: 70th Motorized Rifle Brigade had three.

At least one division in Afghanistan has at least one combined-arms brigade as a subordinate unit in addition to its normal regiments.

Pre-war, the 103rd Guards Airborne Division was at Vitebsk, Belorussian Military District; the 5th Guards Motorized Rifle Division was at Kizyi Arvat, Turkestan Military District; the 201st Motorized Rifle Division was at Frunze and/or Dushanbe, Central Asia Military District. The 375th Guards Airborne Regiment was part of the 105th Guards Airborne Division, now disbanded, which was based in Fergana, Turkestan Military District. Pre-war, the 108th Motorized Rifle Division may have been stationed at Termez.

In addition to these forces, regiments of the 104th Guards Airborne Division fly in from the Soviet Union to participate in major offensives.

The airfield defences at Jalalabad and Kandahar were each reinforced by a *Raydoviki* battalion in 1984. These are probably part of the *spetsnaz* brigades. The strength of the *spetsnaz* brigades is much less than a motorized rifle brigade.

The war in the northern provinces of Afghanistan is conducted by the divisions based inside the Soviet Union. In addition, many of the air and service support forces used in the fighting are based in the Soviet Union.

Above: Soviet mountain troops in Afghanistan. The Soviets revived their wartime practice of having special units of 'mountain troops' in their order of battle after combat experience showed that normal motorized rifle units lacked training and capability. These mountain troops are probably battalions from motorized rifle and airborne divisions that have received the specialized training and equipment that was lacking early in the war. The Resistance consider such units indistinguishable from *spetsnaz*.

been replaced by serving conscripts. Apart from labour units – always heavily Asian – Soviet units in Afghanistan generally have no one ethnic group predominating, although the Baltic States and the western Ukraine seem to provide more than their share of manpower. Service in the Soviet forces is harsh any-where, and Afghanistan is no exception, leading to serious morale and drug abuse problems, especially in non-combatant units.

Until probably about 1984, the Limited Contingent of Soviet Forces in Afghanistan received a twice-yearly turnover with untrained personnel being sent to the units much as in, for example, Group of Soviet Forces Germany. Since then, the Soviets send combat-arms soldiers bound for Afghanistan through a six-month course in a training division in the Soviet Union.

The Kabul Regime in Soviet Tactics, 1978–88

The uniformed, regular Kabul regime forces: the Army, Air and Air Defence Force, Sarandoy (successors to the pre-war Gendarmerie, a light infantry internal security force), Border Troops, police and some militia have carried the burden of much of the war. The effectiveness of Kabul regime forces has become a much more important question since the start of the Soviet withdrawal. For much of the war, these forces were the intermediate and most substantial layer in the three-layer pattern of Soviet military defence against the Resistance, the Kabul regime irregulars being the outermost screen and the Soviets themselves defending the innermost objectives.

The Kabul regime carried the burden of fighting in the border areas in 1978–88. Even when Soviet forces had to be committed in large numbers to the border fighting, as in the relief of Barikot and the attempted relief of Khost, both in 1985, the bulk of the forces have been from the regime. In the face of a better armed and more competent Resistance in 1985–6, they did not start to collapse until the 1987 defeat at Aghandhab, and even then it did not spread throughout the country.

Kabul regime forces, frequently deployed in static garrisons from divisions to companies, are often the target of guerrilla raids and sieges. The Kabul regime troops emerge from their garrisons for sweeps or convoy escort. Major offensives included columns from one or more Kabul regime divisions, either operating in conjunction with Soviet units or acting independently, often with Soviet troops in overwatch positions to prevent desertions and to minimize Soviet casualties. Kabul regime infantry normally marches, though it can be lifted by trucks or APCs. Their tanks are dug into static defences, or used either for infantry support or as convoy escorts. Armoured brigades have been used as complete formations. The Soviets used Kabul regime units to defend vulnerable objectives and, on the offensive, to attack guerrilla positions.

Kabul regime irregular forces include militia and WAD, the intelligence service which runs networks of agents and informers. The Soviets have tried to create and use a multi-source intelligence network, and WAD is the source most feared by the Resistance, but by 1988 the Resistance had won the intelligence war.

The extensive use of militias in addition to uniformed forces is another of the attempts to build on existing Afghan loyalties and divisions. The Kabul regime militia has been a force suitable for interdiction and as an intelligence source, either with combined arms offensives or special operations forces, and their availability in peripheral areas reduces Soviet involvement and hence casualties. Militias have been used to pressure Pakistan, but throughout the war, the militia's willingness to take Communist money has far exceeded their willingness to fight.

Losses

On 25 May 1988, the Soviets announced their total combat losses in Afghanistan to be 13,310 killed in action, 35,478 wounded in action, and 311 missing. They released no information on their counting system. It appears likely that deaths from accidents, wounds or disease are not included. Kabul regime losses are claimed at over 200,000 but probably were three to four times that of the Soviets, although with a much higher percentage of deserters to killed.

The Air War

The Soviet war in Afghanistan has been, in large part, an air war. In addition to operating from bases in the Soviet Union at Mary, Termez, Kushka and Dushanbe, main operating bases in Afghanistan include Shindand (the largest airbase), Bagram, Kabul International (Afghan helicopters and Soviet airlift), Mazar-e-Sharif, Kandahar, and Jalalabad.

The war started with the Soviet airlift into Kabul, and throughout the war, with the Resistance controlling much of the countryside, airlift has been vital; a large percentage of Soviet airlift capability has been devoted to Afghanistan.

Preliminary bombardments before Soviet offensives can involve large-scale airstrikes. Most airstrikes, however, have not been part of combined arms offensives; many have been part of the tactics of de-population. Other airstrikes, by both fighter-bombers and helicopters, have been used for interdiction, attacking Resistance convoys or their way-points.

Fighter-bomber attacks throughout the war have been aimed at minimizing risk to the aircraft. This has greatly reduced accuracy throughout the war, and has been exacerbated since Stinger SAMs were introduced in 1986. After this, fighter-bombers attacked from above 20,000 feet, and so could hit very little.

Helicopters and fighter-bombers fly reconnaissance missions, often armed. Attacks on targets of opportunity were limited throughout much of the war, however. More common are twin-engine

---

TOTAL SOVIET TROOP STRENGTH, FEBRUARY 1988

110,000	Army troops in Afghanistan.
30,000	Army troops fighting in Afghanistan, based in USSR.
3.000	Air Force personnel in Afghanistan.
7,000	Air Force personnel in USSR.
50,000	Support troops in USSR.
2,000	Advisers to Kabul Regime.

On 15 May 1988 Soviet sources gave their troop strength in Afghanistan as 103,300. Their counting rules were not revealed. In addition, there are substantial MVD and KGB forces involved – probably 5,000 troops on both sides of the border, plus several thousand civilian advisers.

In the early stages of the war, there were more than 100 Cuban advisers, civilian and military, though most of these had been withdrawn by 1984–5. There were also more than 100 East German police advisers in the early 1980s. Bulgarians, in uncertain numbers, have been involved. There were persistent unconfirmed reports of Cuban, Ethiopian, Vietnamese, South Yemeni and Syrian troops serving with the Soviet forces.

Right: A Soviet offensive
of the 1982–4 period,
slow, methodical,
following preliminary
bombardments and
airstrikes, establishing
firebases to support each
step of the advance.
What distinguishes this
from some of the earlier
operations, however, is
the use of heliborne
forces (indicated by
parachute symbols) to
cordon off the objective
before the ring was
tightened. These
offensives did not go up
into the mountains, after
the Resistance, but
concentrated on villages
near the roads.

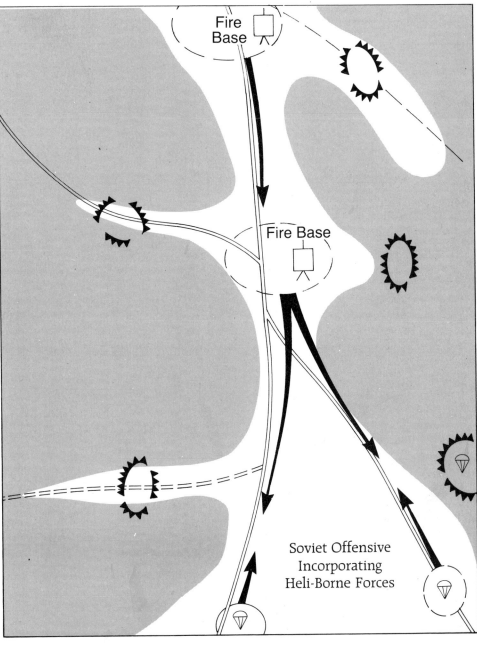

Fire Base

Fire Base

Soviet Offensive
Incorporating
Heli-Borne Forces

Antonov turboprops, equipped with a
variety of sensors, that fly above surface-to-
air missile range throughout much of
Afghanistan. These, like similarly equipped
Hook and Hip helicopters, can also act as
master bombers during air attacks.

The Soviets have also used four and twin
turboprop transports as airborne command
posts during offensives. For tactical actions,
helicopters may be used in the same role.
Transport aircraft are also used to drop flares
at night.

In a Third World country with a limited
road net and rough terrain, the helicopter is
the only effective way for a modern army to
achieve mobility. 'Give a hundred men
helicopters and that will do the work of a
thousand. . . . A battalion with six Wessex
helicopters was worth more to me than a
brigade without them.' The words of
General Sir Walter Walker, Commander-in-
Chief of British and Commonwealth forces
during the Borneo Confrontation, apply to
the Soviet experience in Afghanistan.

IN COMBAT: THE SOVIET HELICOPTER FORCE

Even before the invasion there were more than 100 Soviet helicopters in Afghanistan as well as numbers of DRA-marked aircraft. Throughout the war, Hinds have been used for close air support, for bombing villages, for convoy escort, patrolling and, especially in 1985–6, attacking Resistance supply convoys and their resting and staging areas. In 1979–80 Hinds would often engage at low speeds and altitudes; diving attacks – using machine-guns, 57mm rockets, cluster and HE 250kg bombs – would also be made from a height of 1,000 metres, ending in a sharp evasive turn or low-level repositioning for another pass. Four to eight Hinds would attack in a circular pattern, similar to the American 'wagonwheel' used in Vietnam or the 'circle of death' used by Soviet Il-2 *Sturmoviki* in the Second World War. The regular patterns, however, gave Afghans a break after each attack to scramble to another position.

By late 1980, scout helicopters were used for target acquisition. The Hind or Hip scout ships – carrying the formation commander – would often stay high, out of range of the target, but with visibility. In the *Zapad-81* manoeuvres these tactics were also used, among the first tactics developed in Afghanistan to be transplanted to European conditions.

Responsiveness, integration with the ground forces and tactical flexibility were all frequently lacking throughout much of the war. Soviet Press reports have included accounts of Hind units flying into known concentrations of anti-aircraft weapons, failing to take evasive action when fired on, and attacking positions that the enemy had clearly vacated. Targets of opportunity were seldom attacked. But, motivated by these failures and increasing Resistance air defence, Soviet helicopters changed tactics.

Self-preservation motivated many of the changes. By 1981, Hinds were using low-level flight. By 1983, Hinds and Hips were seen ejecting flares from automatic dispensing systems and would make spiralling approaches to beleaguered outposts. By 1986, hot-brick infra-red jammers and large shrouding systems had been fitted to exhausts to cut down the heat emissions which attract infra-red missiles. The improved crew protection and the armoured bellies of the Hind-D and E models have made them more survivable.

Offensive tactics changed as well. By 1983, Hind attacks would start 7,000 to 8,000 metres away from the targets, running in at low altitude. As soon as they are within range, they open fire with rockets or ATGMS, rising to 20 to 100 metres altitude to fire, often not closing within 1,500 metres of Resistance heavy machine-guns. In other attacks, a flight of Hinds would send one helicopter in at high altitude to draw fire while its wingman remained low, behind a ridge line, ready to attack anyone who opened fire. Night missions, rare before 1983, became common in 1984–5 when attacks would be made using the Hind's optics.

As with all Soviet weapons systems, helicopters are intended to operate as part of a combined arms force. Outpost detachments are landed by helicopter to secure heights until a column passes and are then lifted out. Other battalion-sized forces have been inserted as airborne forward detachments or 'stop groups'. In 1985 offensives, tribal militia were reportedly air inserted by helicopter to secure high ground for Soviet forces. Hinds often worked in co-operation with Hips carrying troops; the troops can either be inserted first, to set up an ambush and call in the Hinds, or brought in to follow up after a Hind attack.

By 1984, almost all major Soviet road convoys had helicopter escort, as do major troop columns during offensives. The Soviet use of preparatory airstrikes before even small-scale ground operations has been applied to convoys as well, striking about six kilometres in distance ahead of the convoy and starting more than an hour before the convoy arrived. The Afghans, however, used this safe area and would wait well back until the convoy was almost level with the chosen ambush site before moving into position. Soviet convoys would also have two or four Hinds overhead or moving in front of the convoy, using reconnaissance by fire against suspected ambush positions. Convoys were also supported by helicopters on alert at nearby airfields, directly 'netted in' to Air Force personnel who accompany the convoy. If ambushed, convoys would call the escorting Hinds back for direct support. If possible, the Soviets would establish a pattern-eight with about six Hinds. The normal Hind attack is four to sixteen aircraft, but three- and five-ship elements of Hinds have been used in Afghanistan, with the odd aircraft being the scout and command helicopter.

PFM-1 'butterfly' mines have been dropped by helicopters throughout Afghanistan, as

Below: The business end of an Mi-8 Hip-E attack helicopter. Even transport Hips are usually armed in Afghanistan, and Mi-8s also flew attack missions until about 1984, when increasing Resistance air defence led to Hinds taking over this mission exclusively. (US Department of Defense)

an interdiction method, to help destroy rural agriculture and, in conjunction with ground forces, to help cordon off villages being swept.

Hip and Hind reconnaissance patrols were at first flown by single ships on a fixed route, often at fixed times, at 100–200m altitude. By 1983–4, the Soviets had made helicopter reconnaissance more effective.

Hooks lifted artillery into the Panjshir Valley during both the 1982 and 1984 offensives, took part in heliborne assaults and were used to insert BMDs for mechanized raids on Resistance supply routes.

In 1986–7, there were about 275 Soviet helicopters based in Afghanistan and another 100 operating from the Soviet Union in support of the war. Of the approximately 1,000 aircraft lost in Afghanistan by 1987, more than 80 per cent have been helicopters. About a third of those lost have been Hinds. Half the helicopters lost have been due to operational accidents while a number of the others have been lost to Resistance attacks on the ground.

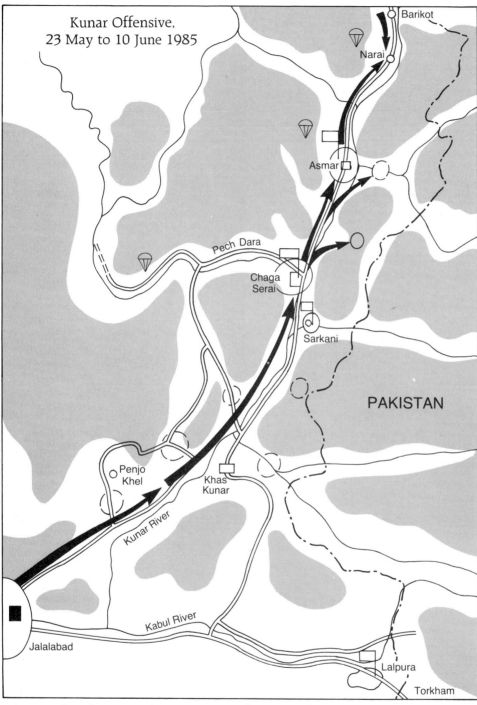

Kunar Offensive,
23 May to 10 June 1985

Barikot
Narai
Asmar
Pech Dara
Chaga
Serai
Sarkani
PAKISTAN
Penjo
Khel
Khas
Kunar
Kunar River
Kabul River
Jalalabad
Lalpura
Torkham

Left: The Kunar Offensive of summer 1985, shows how one Soviet column slowly pushed up the road, linking up with DRA garrisons en route, until it reached the besieged DRA Brigade at Barikot, which made a break-out to meet the column. It also shows how Soviet outposts were established on high ground on the flanks of the column and how airborne forces were inserted by helicopter on the flanks.

Helicopters have been critical to Communist military operations. They have resupplied positions where convoys could never have fought their way through. They have evacuated casualties and, in 1988, garrisons. The Soviets have used battalion-sized or smaller airmobile operations both independently and in conjunction with combined arms forces, usually 10–20km but occasionally up to 50km beyond major Soviet formations.

Helicopters have been used for close air support almost exclusively: fighter-bombers are rarely used to support troops in contact. Helicopters can be responsive to developing tactical situations. Until the Stingers limited their use, major Soviet convoys had Hind

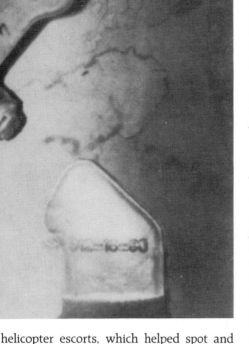

Narrow valleys often limit manoeuvrability and restrict evasive action. Mountains frequently block radio transmissions, forcing the use of relay aircraft. Nevertheless, helicopters have landed troops on mountain crests to secure them for the passage of troop columns or convoys in the valley below.

Weapons

During the course of the war the Soviet and Kabul regime forces used several generations of Soviet-made weapons, including some with field modifications to meet Afghan conditions. Many weapons not in the reference books have turned up in action in Afghanistan. Since 1983–4, Afghanistan has been a priority area for Soviet equipment and many units have been reinforced beyond their 'normal' tables of organization.

The Soviet Army is an armoured army, even in Afghanistan. T-55 main battle tanks came in with the initial invasion, later to be supplemented by T-62s. T-55 and T-62 tanks, like the BMP infantry combat vehicles, have had fabric armour skirts,

helicopter escorts, which helped spot and defeat Resistance ambushes. Helicopter minelaying, especially with PFM-1 'butterfly' mines, has been used for interdiction and as part of tactical blocking forces.

Mountain operations present difficulties for Soviet helicopters. They are often fired on from above, as they fly down valleys.

Above: PFM-1 'butterfly' mines such as these have been dropped throughout Afghanistan. Based on the design of the US BLU-43/44 'Dragontooth', they can last for up to six months before self-detonating. Even picking up a PFM-1 in the pre-detonation stage of its life-cycle will make it explode. (David C. Isby)

AIR ORDER OF BATTLE: FEBRUARY 1988

Soviet fighters: Ten 15-aircraft squadrons in Afghanistan, with an equal number in the Soviet Union supporting operations.

Soviet helicopters: About seven 30–50-aircraft regiments and several independent flights and squadrons, with more than 275 helicopters based in Afghanistan and probably 50 per cent more in the Soviet Union.

Fighters include squadrons of MiG-23 and MiG-27 Flogger, MiG-21 Fishbed, Su-17 Fitter-D, Su-25 Frogfoot. Most Soviet helicopters are Mi-8/Mi-17 Hip, with a quarter being Mi-24 Hind and smaller numbers of Mi-6 Hook and Mi-26 Halo.

One squadron of Frogfoots were at both Shindand and Bagram in 1987–8; more came from the Soviet Union for operations, two squadrons for the 1987–8 relief of Khost. In 1985–6, there was a Fishbed squadron at Kandahar, although by 1987–8 these may have been replaced. There were two squadrons or more of swing-wing fitters at Bagram, Shindand, and Mazar-e-Sharif in 1987–8. By 1987–8, Soviet combat aircraft had left Kabul International, although this, along with Mazar-e-Sharif and Bagram, is a centre of the Soviet airlift effort. Heavy bombers have been based in the Soviet Union throughout the war. Mainly Tu-16 Badger (including, reportedly, some from Naval Aviation), some were used in 1980–1, an increased number, perhaps 24, for operations against Herat and Kandahar in 1983, and two full regiments in 1984. In 1987, a small number, perhaps a squadron, were flying regular operations from Mary. Tu-26 Backfires were introduced to combat in November 1988, hitting targets near Kandahar, while thirty MiG-27 Floggers reinforced Shindand at the same time.

additional plates on the turret, hull and belly installed during the 1984–6 period and have carried them thereafter. T-72s have also seen action, a few earlier in the war, but larger numbers by 1988. The Kabul regime had T-34s, T-54As and T-62s pre-war, and these have suffered heavy losses. For APCs, the Kabul regime started off with BTR-152 APCs in limited numbers; these have suffered losses, and have been partly replaced by BTR-60PB APCs and BRDM-2 scout cars (also used by the Soviets).

Soviet motorized rifle regiments came into Afghanistan riding in standard wheeled BTR-60PB APCs. These have since been replaced by the product-improved versions, the BTR-70 and BTR-80, but all retain the same basic layout and 14.5mm heavy machine-gun armament. BTR-80s have extra stand-off armour attached directly to the hull. Some motorized rifle units used BMP-1 and, starting about 1982, 30mm-armed BMP-2 infantry fighting vehicles, which by 1987 had replaced most of the Soviet BMP-1s. The BMP-1 is also used by the Kabul regime Army.

During the 1979 invasion the Soviet paratroops brought their BMD airborne infantry fighting vehicles with them. These have seen limited combat throughout the war. The paratroops' ASU-85 airborne assault guns, used in the 1979 invasion, saw little combat and were apparently withdrawn fairly early in the war, replaced by the 2S9 120mm SP mortars which were in action by 1982.

Throughout most of the war, the Soviet divisions in Afghanistan kept their tank regiments over the border, garrisoned in the Soviet Union, to deploy when needed for convoy escort and specific offensives. In Afghanistan, armour was used in convoy escort, static defence – BMPs and BTRs being used in both as light tanks, without a rifle squad – and in combined arms offensives; both large- and small-scale, these have been spearheaded by tanks. The elevation limit of Soviet tank guns has proven critical in mountainous terrain, which has led to the use of guntrucks, ZSU-23-4 self-propelled anti-aircraft guns and self-propelled (SP) howitzers in place of tanks in such terrain.

Left: This photograph was taken by the driver of a Soviet Army mail truck, caught out of convoy by the Resistance. It underlines the vulnerability of Soviet logistics in Afghanistan: their truck drivers have frequently had to fight their way through.

Right: Soviet supply convoys have been subject to ambush throughout the war; here a MAZ-500 tank truck burns. If the Soviets were ever to withdraw from their outposts along the Salang Highway, the Kabul regime would probably find it impossible to bring sufficient petrol, oil and lubricants in to sustain a long-term war effort. (Committee for a Free Afghanistan)

Left: A Soviet BMP-1 on convoy escort duty. The large storage box on the rear deck is common. Some Soviet vehicle crews carry the comforts of home – including chairs and rugs – around with them on their rear decking. (Committee for a Free Afghanistan)

Even though Resistance anti-tank capability was limited, it is reported that in the first year of the war Soviet tank units were committed to battle without motorized rifle support and suffered heavy losses.

Artillery has played an increasingly important role throughout the war. The Kabul regime uses a variety of old 76.2mm weapons, and every garrison taken yields a few field or mountain guns. Kabul regime regular units rely increasingly on the towed D-30 122mm howitzer, replacing the earlier M-30 version which they used throughout much of the war. The Soviet motorized rifle divisions which crossed the border in 1979

also brought M-30s with them, but these were replaced first by D-30s, then in part by SO-122 2S1 SP 122mm howitzers. SO-152 2S3 SP 152mm howitzers are also used by the Soviets, together with D-1 towed 152mm howitzers. The Soviet heavy artillery brigade in Afghanistan originally used the long-range 130mm M-46 towed field gun, but by 1987 these had been replaced by SP-152 2S5 SP 152mm guns. The Kabul regime has used 132mm BM-13 multiple rocket-launchers throughout the war. The Soviets have used BM-21a 40-tube and BM-21b 36-tube 122mm and BM-22 220mm multiple rocket-launchers. The BM-22

220mm MRL was introduced by 1984, but the numbers increased greatly in 1986–7, as they took over many missions previous carried out by Hind helicopters, now limited by Stinger SAMs. Known as the 'BM-40' to the Afghans, because they believe it has a 40km range, the BM-22 fires high-explosive rockets as well as those carrying minelets, or incendiary or fragmentation sub-munitions.

Soviet mortars include a few of the big SM-240 2S4 SP 240mm mortars, 82mm automatic 2B9 Vasilyek, 120mm M-1943 and 82mm M-1937 types, the latter two also used by the Kabul regime.

A wide range of anti-tank weapons are used, often against Afghan houses and

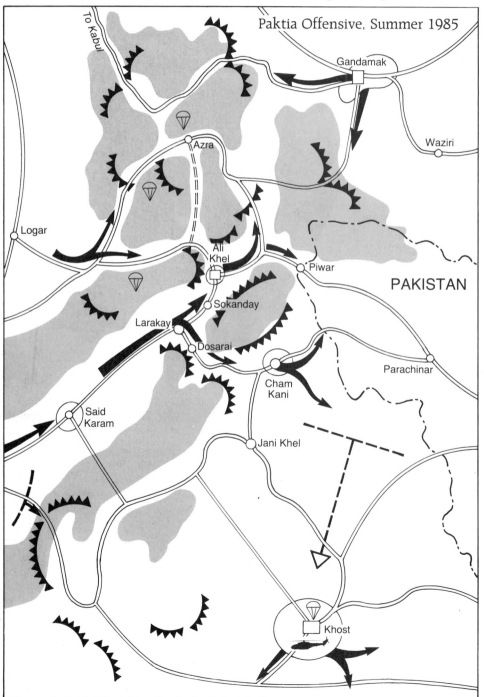

Paktia Offensive, Summer 1985

Left: The 1985 Summer Offensive into Paktia shows a number of key elements of Soviet offensive operations in Afghanistan:
– the use of multiple axes of advance.
– the offensive use of encircled forces (at Khost and Ali Khel) in co-operation with relief columns in 'hammer and anvil' tactics.
– the insertion of battalion-sized forces by helicopter (indicated by parachute symbol) to seize high ground. Some of these forces were DRA militia.
The dashed arrows represent the subsequent part of the operation, which was never carried out.
When the Soviets relieved Khost in 1988, the offensive went directly from Gardez.

WHAT HAS THE SOVIET MILITARY LEARNED FROM AFGHANISTAN

Although the war it has fought in Afghanistan is very different from what it was prepared for, the Soviet Army appears to have learned some real and legitimate lessons. Indeed, if the Soviets ever cross another frontier, it is more likely to be in southern Asia than in western Europe or Manchuria, where nuclear escalation could soon follow, and the lessons of Afghanistan would be directly applicable. The Soviets themselves have already stated that their officers are being instructed by Afghanistan veterans. A whole range of elements, from helicopter tactics, to physical training, to the weeding out of officers whose capabilities looked sterling on paper but who failed the test of combat, are at work. It can be compared with John Masters' description, in *Bugles and a Tiger*, of the lessons learned from fighting on the then-British side of the Durand Line: 'From the Frontier itself we learned unwinking, unsleeping, alertness. From the Pathans we learned more about the tactical value of ground than any of our competitors or future enemies knew.'

sangars: rocket-propelled grenades RPG-7 (with the OG-7 HE-Frag round), RPG-16, RPG-18, and RPG-22; AT-3 Sagger and AT-4 Spigot Anti-Tank Guided Missiles (ATGMs). Soviet RPO-A and RPO-50 flame rockets are carried not only by engineers but by heli-borne forces as well.

Infantry weapons are vital in any counter-insurgency war. Standard Soviet 5.45mm infantry weapons are used: AK-74 and AKS-74 rifles, AKSU carbines, RPK light machine-guns. The increase of the use of special operations forces in 1984–6 also meant the introduction of silenced weapons: both 7.62mm AKMS rifles and 9mm P6 pistols. The Kabul regime forces mainly used 7.62mm weapons – AK-47, AKM, AKMS rifles, RPK light machine-guns – although they are also receiving 5.45mm weapons. 7.62mm SVD snipers' rifles (the numbers of which have been tripled to nine per company in Afghanistan), PKM 7.62mm general-purpose machine-guns and 12.7mm NSV (replacing DShKM) heavy machine-guns are also used.

Soviet grenade-launchers include 30mm weapons, mounted on tripods (the AGS-17), on BTRs and BMPs, and in the nose of Mi-8/17 helicopters. The 40mm BG-15 grenade-launcher fits under the barrel of assault rifles.

In the mid-1980s, the Soviets were using a wide range of high-technology systems in Afghanistan. There have been repeated reports of the limited use of FROG-7 rockets or SS-21 and, in 1988, SS-1 *Scud* surface-to-surface missiles using conventional high-explosive or sub-munition warheads. Improved night optics have also been seen, used by helicopters, infantrymen and observation posts.

Extensive use has been made of incendiary bombs: white phosphorus, napalm and fuel air explosive. Soviet high-explosive bombs, old design 57mm rockets, and cluster bomb units are the most widely used munitions. They suffer from a high dud rate yet such old-technology weapons far outnumber the laser-guided bombs and other sophisticated munitions used in Afghanistan. Many Kabul regime pilots tend to drop their bombs unarmed. Laser-guided bombs were used against targets in caves, especially in the 1986 Zhawar offensive. Fuel-air explosive, which creates a tremendous over-pressure, was used against similar targets as well as minefields. Increased numbers of Su-25 Frogfoots, capable of accurate weapons delivery, were seen after 1984. Known to the Afghans as the 'German jet' (on the grounds that it is as superior to Soviet-made fighter-bombers as German-made consumer goods are superior to Soviet-made consumer goods), it became the most hated aircraft in Afghanistan.

Mines have been extensively used by both sides. The Soviets used two million mines in the 1985 eastern border campaign alone, mainly for large-scale interdiction, to extend control beyond direct fire range. These were mainly the PFM-1 'butterfly' mine, which has exacted a terrible toll from

Right: Soviet bombs have an extremely high dud rate, and their casings are found throughout Afghanistan. These three Afghans are *en route* to a scrap dealer in Pakistan. (David C. Isby)

Afghan civilians and animals. When the Soviets started withdrawing from their bases in 1988, they neither removed their minefields, nor reported their locations. This assured heavy loss of life to mines for years to come.

The use of chemical weapons has been seen at different points in the war, starting before the Soviet invasion. There is clear and convincing evidence of the use of chemical weapons, including physical samples. High-technology chemical agents, such as tricothecene toxin ('yellow rain') and nerve agents were used on a limited and apparently non-systematic basis early in the war. The evidence of chemical warfare use includes two samples of 'yellow rain' brought to the west in captured gas masks, the filming of a chemical warfare attack (and its victims), by Bernd de Bruijn, a Dutch journalist, and repeated reports from Afghan sources and doctors in Pakistan. Those coming from inside Afghanistan would not be able to prepare 'cover stories' in collaboration with those already in Pakistan. There are no confirmed cases of their use after 1982. Phosgene was used at least until

1984, when casualties were treated inside Afghanistan by an American, Doctor Robert Simon, assistant professor at UCLA Medical School. Non-lethal agents, including CS, CN and a non-lethal incapacitant, have been more widely used.

Above: A Soviet Su-25 Frogfoot fighter-bomber pulls up after an attack on an Afghan target. Under its nose, it mounts a laser target designator for use with precision-guided munitions. These were used to drop bombs on cave mouths in the 1986 Zhawar fighting. (US Department of Defense)

BATTLES FOR THE BORDER, 1978–88

From the beginning of the war, many battles have centred around the various border forts, many of which held out under intermittent siege, until the Soviet withdrawal started in May 1988.

Many of these forts were built around old pre-war structures, dating back to the Anglo-Afghan Wars. Pre-war, they were garrisoned to keep an eye on trade and smuggling and to bring the power of Kabul to the locals. Throughout the war, however, with their Kabul regime garrisons they have been key elements in Soviet operations along the borders.

The forts block supply routes (because they are normally located in valleys, along roads, or at choke points), and provide not only a visible Communist presence, but are also useful for target acquisition. They act as communications centres, for both the military and the WAD's extensive Human Intelligence (HUMINT) nets.

Border forts have been a Resistance target since early in the war and have functioned as a magnet for Resistance activity, absorbing efforts that would otherwise have been applied closer to Soviet-occupied positions. Resistance attacks on such positions also concentrated their own forces, making them a better target for Soviet air and artillery attack.

Because they were manned by Kabul regime forces, often militia, with only Soviet advisers, they represented a low level of investment, but many of them became dependent on air resupply early in the war. Improved Resistance anti-aircraft capability made such resupply flights too costly to be sustained and from 1987 the Soviets – leaving the Kabul regime behind – have pulled their own forces out of a number of more isolated positions in the interior. But until May 1988, despite the Stinger threat, the Kabul regime border forts held on and were only abandoned as the Soviets began to withdraw. Few were taken by Resistance assault.

4. THE KABUL REGIME

Leadership and Government

In 1978–88, the Republic of Afghanistan, suffered the same disunity and low level of organizational skills that has plagued the Resistance, but it lacked its nationwide success of motivation, ideology and nationalism. Gorbachev, conscious of his client's limitations, characterized the Kabul regime not as a socialist nation but as 'a state in the national democratic stage of development'.

The head of state, Najibullah, was installed in power in 1986, replacing his predecessor Babrak Karmal. A medical doctor, he made his reputation as head of the KHAD in 1980–5. He is widely believed to have been a KGB asset for many years

before the war. Najibullah, like his predecessor, presides over a government made up of both his own *Parcham* and the *Khalq* Communist parties, and which had further fragmented during his administration. No one has forgotten the *Khalq* purges in 1978–9, which Najibullah, like Karmal, escaped by being exiled as ex-ambassador, not that Najibullah was used to exact revenge on many *Khalqis*. Despite – or rather possibly because of – his hard-line reputation, Najibullah was intended by the Soviets to implement policies introduced under Karmal with less hesitation and more force against the Resistance and their supporters, but at the same time trying to put together a broad-based pro-regime coalition.

Events, as so often in Afghanistan, did not work out the way Moscow intended. As fragmentation and in-fighting in the PDPA increased in 1986–8, the splits in the Afghan

Right: Kabul regime paratroopers are trucked through Kabul in the annual military parade. While the paratroops were at first considered as 'élite' troops, they never recovered from their 1980 mutiny and have been largely limited to airfield security. The commando units include airborne-trained troops as well.

military and religious establishments loyal to Kabul, which Karmal had succeeded in balancing, re-opened with a more complex network of competing loyalties set up around individual members of the Kabul regime leadership.

Even the pro-Soviet Afghans cannot achieve unity, although the Soviets dominate the Kabul regime economically and politically. The Soviets are often reduced to trying to threaten the leadership into obedience. This only underlines the fact that Soviet control over the Afghan Communists has never been complete, despite their extensive attempts to implement control by economic integration (especially of the north), the adviser system, and a whole network of relations: army to army, secret police to secret police, party to party, Politburo to Politburo and, again especially in the north, local government to local government and commercial state enterprise to commercial state enterprise.

Najibullah failed to increase domestic or international legitimacy and support. In both cases, this attempt has been framed largely in Islamic terms. Najibullah, like Karmal, has made a show of respecting Islam and traditional institutions, funding any religious figures willing to swear loyalty to the regime. This has been evident since the invasion: Karmal's first speech to the Afghan people, made while he was still in the Soviet Union, started by invoking the name of God as a Muslim head of state. This stands in contrast to the repression of both religion and custom, and the purging of those who believed in both, that marked the Taraki regime.

But years of evolving polical and diplomatic tactics have still not succeeded in establishing the regime's Islamic credentials with the majority of Afghans or the Muslim world. The Kabul regime's Islamic supporters – Syria, South Yemen, the PLO – are also those most dependent on Soviet support.

Below: Party-political work in a Kabul regime Army unit. The PDPA control over the armed forces has never been anywhere near as complete as that in Soviet and east European armies and a number of senior officers throughout the 1980–8 period remained non-party members.

Right: Kabul regime *agitprop* activities in a village. In 1986–7 both the Soviets and the Kabul regime increased these 'hearts and minds' actions, but they had little additional success in the villages.

Below right: Kabul regime militia, demonstrating the extreme youth of some members, the assortment of weapons, and the absence of field equipment.

Above left: Resistance 122mm artillery, such as this M-30 howitzer, suffers from a shortage of ammunition and frequent mis-allocation of trained artillerymen. (Committee for a Free Afghanistan)

Left: This T-55 was knocked out by the RPG-7 gunner standing on it. The RPG-7 has become a favourite Resistance weapon, not only against tanks but as an all-purpose source of firepower. (Committee for a Free Afghanistan)

Armed Forces

The Kabul regime military dealt effectively with traditional local revolts and the first Islamicist risings of the 1970s, but started to collapse in 1978–9. In 1978, the Afghan Army had a nominal strength of 110,000 and an actual strength of about 80,000; by the end of 1980, it was down to about 20,000.

Throughout the war, personnel strength has been one of the critical problems of the Kabul regime's military forces. By 1988, the army had a maximum strength of about 35–40,000, with an annual loss of about 10,000 men through desertion, demobilization and casualties. Conscription is by press-gang, which are not particular about age or prior service. Mutinies resulted when conscript service was extended from three to four years in March 1984. The manpower pool the Kabul regime has to draw from is limited to the cities and those areas of the countryside which the Communist forces sweep. Finding men to lead such a force has been a problem. The Kabul regime's officers and NCOs include some committed Communists, who believe in it as their brothers in the hills believe in Islam, but more of them are opportunists or outright thugs. Others play the dangerous game of double agent, supplying information and supplies to the Resistance. Since 1981, the Kabul regime has paid its officers and NCOs well by Afghan standards. Political reliability is a prime qualification, and education is not, so many Kabul regime junior officers are illiterate; but the PDPA never achieved the penetration and control of the military that Communist governments have achieved elsewhere, despite the fact that Soviet-style political officers were instituted by the mid-1980s.

Left: Desertion has plagued all aspects of the regime's armed forces since 1978. These deserters – some have shed their uniforms, others retain them – were heading to rejoin families in refugee camps in Pakistan in 1987. Many would then return to the war on the side of the Resistance; others would stay in the camps or look for work in Pakistan. The Resistance would traditionally give deserters a few rupees for food for the journey, but in 1987 there were so many that the money ran out. (David C. Isby)

Left: Kabul regime infantry in the field – a photograph taken by a soldier who later joined the Resistance. (National Islamic Front of Afghanistan)

Right: ZSU-23-4 SP AA gun of the Kabul regime Army. The Afghans had a limited number of these pre-war, but almost all were lost in action within a few years and not replaced.

Right: BTR-60PB APC of the Kabul regime Army. These have replaced many of the earlier BTR-152s as they were lost in combat. Petrol-powered, they often 'brew-up' if mined, but they occasionally limp out of a minefield even if one or two wheels are missing.

Right: BTR-152 APC of the Kabul regime Army. These were supplied pre-war, as part of the continuing relationship between the Soviets and the Afghan military. The service that was traditionally most dependent on the Soviet relationship, however, was the Air and Air Defence Force which in 1978–80, proved to be generally more supportive of the regime than the Army.

The Kabul regime armed forces of 1988 were resistant to generalization. Desertion remains a major factor and probably over half of the conscripts would desert if given the opportunity. The Kabul regime tries to send conscripts away from their home area to discourage desertions, and the dense minefields around many outposts has the dual effect of keeping them in as well as keeping the Resistance out. A minority, motivated by ideology, opportunism, military discipline or tribal loyalty, often fight as hard as their opponents, and with more organization. This kept more than a handful of minor and all major Kabul regime positions from falling from 1980 until 1988. Indeed, after the collapse of 1978–80, the Kabul regime suffered many setbacks, but large-scale failures in morale and mass desertions did not start to re-appear until 1987. Even then, there were no whole brigades changing sides (as happened in 1979, in the Kunar) or, until June 1988, no provincial capitals being given over to the Resistance by its garrison (as happened at Faizabad, Badakhshan, in 1979) until 1988.

The quality of Kabul regime forces has differed widely throughout the war. Some, such as the 15th Division in Kandahar and the 17th Division in Herat, have never had much success in dealing with the local Resistance. The 25th Division, garrisoning Khost and other Paktia forts throughout most of the war, has a reputation for hard fighting, but it is unusual in that, since about 1983, it has been officered almost completely from the *Khalq* party.

Tension with the Soviets was common throughout the war. Because the Kabul regime military has many guerrilla sympathizers, the Soviets told them little of planned operations throughout the war. Despite this, the Resistance had advance notice of most major Communist offensives.

Kabul regime units are all understrength. Divisions are normally the size of weak brigades, and 200-man battalions are common. Kabul regime infantry divisions and regiments retain what is, on paper, a triangular organization: three 3-battalion infantry regiments, an artillery regiment, and a tank battalion. In reality, each division's organization is unique. They have become territorial headquarters, com-

manding all the ground forces subordinate to the Ministry of Defence in their assigned sector. When a division is tasked to provide mobile forces, such as for an offensive out of its sector, it will put together a mobile, composite column out of the forces not tied down to local security and garrison missions. Brigades have replaced many of the regiments, being similar smaller composites of all the units in their areas of operations.

The Kabul regime had a number of élite units – the 26th Airborne Battalion and the 444th, 666th, 37th and 38th Commando Brigades. The airborne was élite in name only. Reportedly it was formed from Air Force groundcrews to provide political leverage in 1979. It mutinied in 1980, after the invasion, but was reportedly later reformed. The Commando brigades were originally considered politically reliable and so were used as mobile strike forces. They have suffered heavy losses throughout the war.

The use of multiple armed forces is seen in the Soviet Union and especially in its Warsaw Pact allies. Such forces function as a system of checks and balances on the army.

Above: The mix of young and old in the Kabul regime militia, is also repeated in the uniformed armed forces.

Right: Kabul regime sappers look for mines. Their old-model Soviet mine-detectors do not work against the new plastic mines used by the Resistance, which require sniffer dogs, probes, or large mine-plows. Countermine warfare has been an important element of the Communist war effort in Afghanistan and all major troop movements have included substantial engineer detachments to detect and remove mines.

Right: Kabul regime infantrymen armed with AK-47s, part of a 2,000-man brigade which switched sides in the Kunar Valley in 1979, being inspected by their former commander, Colonel Abdul Rauf. As a result of internal divisions within the Resistance, the advantage presented by this large-scale defection and the influx of modern weapons was not exploited.

Left: A Kabul regime BTR-60PB advances down a narrow valley – a photograph brought over to the Resistance by a rallier. The difficulties of using mechanized forces off the limited road net in Afghanistan is readily apparent, as is the vulnerability of armoured vehicles to mines in defiles. (National Islamic Front of Afghanistan)

Above: A BMP-2 infantry fighting vehicle, armed with a 30mm cannon, of the 70th Motorized Rifle Brigade, near Kandahar. The 70th was one of the few Soviet formations known by number to the Resistance, and had a reputation for hard fighting. It included at least one air assault battalion.

Below: When Soviet paratroops arrived in Afghanistan, they brought their ASU-85 airborne assault guns with them, but since 1979 these have seen little action. Its lack of a turret would have been especially constricting in Afghanistan, where manoeuvring into firing positions is difficult for armoured vehicles. (US Department of Defense)

In the Kabul regime, the divisions within the Communist party have meant that the different armed forces each reflect a different internal political constituency. The different Kabul regime armed forces are difficult to differentiate in action; garrisons are often a mixture of army, various militias, party cadres and WAD.

The most important single Kabul regime force does not wear uniform. It is the WAD (State Security Ministry), the 30–60,000 strong Kabul regime secret police and, effectively, an extension of the KGB. The WAD (formerly, and better known as, KHAD), is one – possibly the only – element of the Kabul regime that works better in 1987–8 than it did in 1980. Its 1988 head, Ghulam Faruq Yaqabi, was originally a protégé of Najibullah, but by 1988 he had emerged as a competitor. In 1987–8, the WAD was conducting, on behalf of the Soviets, the world's largest campaign of state-supported terrorism across the border in Pakistan. Throughout the war, it infil-trated the Resistance and ran networks of spies, informers and assassins. WAD is also responsible for the custody of political prisoners, their interrogation and punishment. The WAD's politics are *Parcham*. Their widespread violence with pro-*Khalq* police and some Army units when Najibullah was in charge contributed to the re-emergence of inter-party fighting in 1986–7. WAD also fields para-military units (many of those of the Ministry of the Interior are under their operational control), and since 1986 has been exerting greater operational control over a broad range of forces.

The largest uniformed force outside the Ministry of Defence is the Sarandoy. These are under the Ministry of the Interior (normally Khalq-controlled), but since Najibullah came to power, they are often under the operational command of the WAD. The Ministry of the Interior, in 1988, has armed forces that total about 30–40,000, almost as large as the army. The successor to the former Gendarmerie, the Sarandoy is made

THE FAILINGS OF AFGHAN ARMIES

The lack of success the Kabul regime army has had in dealing with the Resistance cannot be attributed solely to the strength of their opponents or the unpopularity of the regime, but includes a current running through Afghan life since the nineteenth century and before: 'The Afghan does not lack native courage and in hill warfare he is unrivalled, so long as it takes the shape of guerrilla fighting; but once he is asked to sink his identity and to become merely a unit in a battalion he loses all self-confidence and is apt to think more of getting away than of stubbornly holding his ground as he would have done with his own friends led by his own chief.' – Edward Hensman, 1882.

Above: Kabul regime aircrew with their MiG-17 Frescoe fighter-bombers. These had been withdrawn by 1986, but were extensively used in the early years of the war. While its bombload and accuracy was limited, its pilots liked its low-altitude man-oeuvrability, superior to that of the Su-7 Fitter.

up of serving conscripts, equipped with standard infantry and infantry support weapons and wearing the same basic uniforms as the Army. While it had been primarily committed to the defence of Kabul in 1985–6, in 1987 it deployed more strength into the provinces. It is organized into provincial regiments and, like most Kabul regime armed forces, it has its own militia forces. The police, also under the Ministry of the Interior, provide tactical units as well as standard law-enforcement duties mainly limited to Kabul, Mazar-e-Sharif, Jalalabad and a few other towns.

The Border Troops did not exist before the war. Created in the early days of the war, they were transferred from the Ministry of Tribes and Frontiers to Defence Ministry control in 1983. Like many of the armed forces outside the Ministry of Defence, they were built up as a balance to the Kabul regime army. These forces maintain close links with KGB Border Troops, who provide their advisers and, in the Badakhshan province area, co-operate operationally. They have proven highly unsuccessful. Their outposts along the borders have proven a weak barrier to Resistance infiltration, even

KABUL REGIME AIR FORCE, FEBRUARY 1988

Fighter-bombers: about four regiments, at Bagram (250th Regiment, with Fishbeds), Shindand, and Mazar-e-Sharif. Aircraft include MiG-21 Fishbeds, Su-17 Fitter-Ds, and surviving Su-7 Fitters. The MiG-17 Fresco and MiG-19 Farmers are unlikely to be still in service.

Helicopters: Mi-8/Mi-17 Hips with a quarter to a third of Kabul regime helicopter strength being Mi-25 Hind-Ds and Mi-24 Hind-E/Fs. About 60–80 helicopters, organized into two regiments, at Kabul (377th Regiment) and Mazar-e-Sharif (232nd Regiment).

Transport: Airlift duties are handled by a range of twin-engine Antonov turboprop transports, which have suffered heavily to Stingers, those of the state airline Bakhtar being used interchangeably with Air Force aircraft. In May 1988, the first An-12 Cub four-engined turboprop transports were delivered for a total of 36 to 60 turboprops plus piston-engined Il-14s.

KABUL REGIME ARMY ORDER OF BATTLE

Unit	Location–27 December 1979	Location–February 1988
Army GHQ	Kabul	Kabul
I Corps HQ	Kabul	Kabul
II Corps HQ	Kandahar	Kandahar
III Corps HQ	Gardez	Gardez
4th Armoured Bde	Pul-e-Charki	Pul-e-Charki
7th Armoured Bde	Kandahar	Kandahar
15th Armoured Bde	Pul-e-Charki	Pul-e-Charki
2nd Div (1)	not in OB	Panjshir
7th Div (2)	Kabul	Moqor
8th Div (3)	Kargha, Kabul	Kargha, Kabul
9th Div (4)	Asadabad, Kunar	Asadabad, Kunar
11th Div (5)	Jalalabad	Jalalabad/Samarkhel
12th Div (6)	Gardez	Gardez
14th Div (7)	Ghazni	Ghazni
15th Div (8)	Kandahar	Kandahar
18th Div (9)	Mazar-e-Sharif	Mazar-e-Sharif
17th Div (10)	Herat	Herat
20th Div (11)	Nahrin, Baghlan	Nahrin, Baghlan
25th Div (12)	Khost, Paktia	Khost, Paktia
37th Commando Bde	?	Kabul
38th Commando Bde	?	Kabul
444th Commando Bde	Kabul area	Panjshir?
666th Commando Bde	?	Paktia?
252nd Recon Bn	Kabul	Kabul
212th Recon Bn	Gardez	Gardez
203rd Recon Bn	Kandahar	Kandahar
GHQ Artillery Brigade	Kabul area	Kabul?
880th MRL Brigade	Kabul	Kabul
26th Airborne Bn (13)	Kabul	Bagram
88th SAM Regt (13)	Bagram/Shindand	Bagram/Shindand
99th SAM Regt (13)	Kabul	Kabul
77th ADA Regt (13)	Kabul	Kabul
1st Frontier Bde (14)	not in OB	Jalalabad
2nd Frontier Bde (14)	not in OB	Khost
3rd Frontier Bde (14)	not in OB	Badakshan
4th Frontier Bde (14)	not in OB	Nimruz
5th Frontier Bde (14)	not in OB	Herat area
6th Frontier Bde (14)	not in OB	Paktika
7th Frontier Bde (14)	not in OB	Kandahar
8th Frontier Bde (14)	not in OB	Paktika
9th Frontier Bde (14)	not in OB	Kabul
10th Frontier Bde (14)	not in OB	Kunar
24th Sarandoy Rgt (15)	not in OB	Badakshan

at the height of the anti-infiltration campaign of 1984–6.

Militias – 50–100,000 strong in 1988 – represent the bulk of the Kabul regime's irregular forces. They constitute a broad range of forces and capabilities. Militia recruits – frequently whole tribes or clans fighting under their own leaders – have come, throughout the war, from Pathan tribes with economic links to Kabul or at odds with their neighbours or the Resistance, especially among Afridis, Waziris, Shinwaris and Hill Mohmands on both sides of the Afghanistan–Pakistan border and fighting under their own leaders and in their own way, much like the Resis-

NOTES

Non-divisional units include reconnaissance, engineer and artillery battalions.

1. Formed to command Kabul regime forces in Panjshir Valley. Formed for the Panjshir VIII offensive from one brigade each of the 8th and 20th Divisions and possibly the 444th Commando Brigade. Withdrawn July 1988.

2. Subordinate units include 65th Brigade. Units deployed south of Kabul, around highway to Kandahar and Ghazni, until defeated in June 1988. Mutinied in 1984.

3. Subordinate units include 4th Regiment, 5th Brigade, 72nd Regiment, Maidanshah; has number of AFVs, including BTR-60PB APCs.

4. Subordinate units include 69th Brigade, Asadabad, 55th Brigade, Barikot (withdrawn, May 1988), 71st Regiment, Ghanikhel; 31st Regiment, 46th Regiment. Withdrew to Jalalabad October 1988.

5. Subordinate units include 81st Regiment, Jalalabad airfield; 32nd, 55th, 61st Brigades.

6. Subordinate units include 15th (Urgun), 22nd and 67th Brigades, 6th Regiment.

7. Subordinate units include 3rd Brigade, 28th Regiment, 40th Regiment, Paktia.

8. Subordinate units include 36th Brigade at Naray, 43rd Regiment at Qalat, Zabul Province (until taken by the Resistance, June 1988), and a brigade in the Helmand Valley.

9. Subordinate units include 62nd Regiment, Mazar-e-Sharif, and 35th Regiment, Shebarghan.

10. Area of operations includes Badghis and Ghowr. Subordinate units include 2nd Regiment, 28th Brigade. 1985 strength 900–1,400.

11. Subordinate units include 20th, 23rd, 75th Regiments. Withdrew July 1988.

12. Includes 23rd, 19th, 59th and 6th Artillery Brigades, plus a tank regiment. A heavily *Khalq*, hard-fighting division.

13. Subordinate to the Air and Air Defence Force. Combined strength was two SA-2 (one destroyed in August 1988) and three SA-3 batteries plus elements of one air defence artillery brigade.

14. Unit of the Border Troops.

15. Under Ministry of the Interior Command. There are probably provincial regiments in each Afghan province.

tance. In areas where there is no tribal structure, militias are organized around villages or workplaces. Regime-controlled factories and collective farms often have their own militia, formed from PDPA supporters and hired guards. De-tribalized individuals from cities or towns are also potential militia recruits.

Groups of Resistance fighters who have become displeased with their comrades in arms or their leadership or who have been bought off are among the most effective militia groups, more feared than the usually unenthusiastic Kabul regime regulars. Some Resistance groups that have switched sides have kept their identity as militia in the Kandahar area (under Ismatullah Muslim, one of the few ralliers to the 1985 National Fatherland Front who reportedly achieved operational control of besieged Kandahar in October 1988) and Takhar province. Yet, overall, throughout the war, militias have proven unreliable. While there have been many occasions when they carried the day on the battlefield for the Communists, there have been many more when they took the money and did nothing or supported the guerrillas.

Paktia has the strongest militia strength, followed by Nangarhar and Kabul. Militias do not necessarily operate in their own areas; for instance the militia guarding the Sarobi power lines when these were attacked in June 1987, was from Kandahar. Among the militia operating near Kandahar at the same time were Mari Baluch tribesmen, originally from Pakistan, and a force of Jowzjanis from the north, where militias are strong.

The Kabul regime has encouraged some militia groups to go into farming opium poppies and have marketed their crops, which the Resistance, from religious considerations, will normally not do on a large scale (though the chance for some quick money has certainly found some Resistance takers who can persuade the local mullahs to look the other way).

In addition to the armed forces, armed PDPA cadres are found at all state and party enterprises. 'Revolution Defense Groups' have been formed as a militia-like force under PDPA auspices. The PDPA Pioneers have also been expected to join the war effort. The youth wings of both the Khalq and *Parcham* parties have fielded combat units. Like all Kabul regime forces, quality has varied greatly. They have certainly taken

heavy losses, for these types of units are the most obvious, and the most exposed, manifestation of the Communist regime. Many are no more enthusiastic than the Kabul regime military. Some perform better. A *Parcham* youth wing group styling itself Pasadran (Revolutionary Guards), goaded by accusations of inaction, saw heavy fighting in the Panjshir in 1984. 'Democratic Youth Force' of the PDPA – mostly *Parcham*, some *Khalq* – saw action in the 1987 Jadji offensive. In 1986, two non-party militia organizations were formed: Defa-e-Khudi (Self-Defence) and Defa-e-Mulki (Civil Defence), although apparently these have not apparently proven reliable. In 1988, PDPA members were mobilized in party battle groups.

Above left: Joint civic action: Kabul regime and Soviet troops plant trees. Combined military operations with both armies were commonplace throughout 1980–8.

Above right: The future of Afghanistan after a Soviet withdrawal – indeed, whether the withdrawal is even completed, as agreed in February 1989, depends in large part on how the Kabul regime's uniformed armed forces, like this vehicle park guard, stand up to the Resistance.

5. THE AFGHAN RESISTANCE

The Evolving Resistance

The Afghan Resistance is not an army but rather a people in arms; its strengths and weaknesses are those of Afghan society. While national in scope, it is religious in content; Islam has provided legitimacy and a unifying ideology, enabling deep divisions between groups and individuals to be transcended. The Resistance is organic; it grew rather than was created, unlike movements such as the Viet Minh. The basic composition of the Resistance, of independent villages or strongholds as well as the nature of Afghan life and society, made it self-sufficient compared with other insurgencies. The decentralized Resistance is one reason why there is no single theory of Afghan guerrilla warfare nor a single Afghan Resistance strategy. There is no Afghan equivalent of Mao, Ho Chi Minh, or Kim Il Sung, matching theory and direction with fighting. Part of the reason is the pre-war split between Afghanistan intellectual life, centered almost exclusively in Kabul, and the people in the hills and valleys who have done most of the fighting. In 1987, Resistance active strength was estimated by their own leadership at about 200,000, of whom about half were trained, experienced fighters. They are drawn from a much larger pool of manpower, the remainder being engaged in agriculture, in the refugee camps, or working in the cities or abroad. Other estimates range from 90–120,000 (US sources, 1980–1); to 150,000 (French expert, 1985); to 200,000–250,000 (Western analysis, 1983); to 250,000–330,000 (Afghan sources, 1981–2); 744,000 (Resistance source, 1984) to 200,000 (US source, 1988). Total guerrilla manpower is probably equal to 10 per cent of the population remaining in Afghanistan outside the cities – six to nine million in 1987–8 – so overall manpower shortage has not been a problem, but rather the lack of skilled people, both in technical and organizational terms, has.

If the Soviets started from a relatively low level of tactical competence, the Afghans certainly suffered to a much greater extent. Gerard Challiand, a French expert who has been in the field with many guerrilla movements, wrote in 1981, 'The Afghan insurgents know little of modern revolutionary war – its efficiency or organization or careful planning of time and work.' Since then, starting from the base of the first years of the war, the Afghans have gained the knowledge that Challiand saw they lacked. They learned slowly – many have not learned at all – and paid dearly for it. In 1987–8, despite the boost given by the Stingers and improved battlefield effectiveness, the Afghans did not take a major border garrison or effectively project power into Kabul until the Soviets started to withdraw.

Progress from traditional warrior to modern guerrilla has been much greater in northern Afghanistan – the difference between Ahmad Shah Massoud's forces and any others is substantial – but is certainly not absent even in Pathan areas, despite being divided by tribal loyalties. An example of greater sophistication among the Resistance, even in Pushtu-speaking Afghanistan, is shown by how Hezb-i-Islami (Khalis) deployed the first four 120mm mortars it received in 1987. Rather than parcelling them out to successful commanders as with previous weapons, these were formed into a battery with crews paid a salary and commanded by a proven commander. Having several of the few gunners who can conduct indirect fire, it could move where needed for operations, but technical and supply problems curtailed their use.

Apart from Ahmad Shah Massoud's *motareks* (full-time soldiers, which became the central forces), the Resistance has no divisions or brigades that can move from area to area, although groups will often operate out of their area for specific operations. Regional guerrilla commanders have emerged who can deploy substantial forces, but they must often put together a 'coalition' for each operation, a process which, although never simple, became prevalent as the war continued. Yet too often, instead of thorough planning, different groups would simply move towards the sound of the guns if the political problems had not been resolved.

The religious nature of Resistance leadership and the traditional distrust of the military in Afghan society has limited the Resistance's use of the military knowledge of former officers of the Kabul regime or Royal Army. However, some of the more significant commanders had a military background (Ismael Khan and Sayid Jaglan, for example), and those commanders who do not have such experience often have former officers as advisers.

The Afghans have not always had their best men as leaders. Traditional leadership meant that birth or position – or, alternatively, religious authority or stature – often outweighed competence. Similarly, the traditional Afghan way of making decisions by a *jirga*, or council, is no way to run a war. Western armies abandoned councils of war as a decision-making process in the eighteenth century. Slowness of decision-making is widespread even among successful Resistance commanders, especially those in Pathan areas, such as Jalulladin Haqani.

The realization that fighting is only a small part of the business of a modern guerrilla has dawned slowly on the Afghans. Some leaders such as, for example, Massoud, Ismael Khan, and Amin Wardak have been able to reconcile the requirements of Afghan traditional society, Islamic life and law, and the demands of a guerrilla war. Civil organization and government has become a

Left: Ahmad Shah Massoud (left) stands among his victorious central forces troops. The weapon carried at right is an AKS-74 with a BG-15 grenade-launcher, which has been carried by Soviet heliborne troops to increase their available firepower, together with large numbers of RPG-18 and RPG-22 light anti-tank weapons (LAWs) and RPO-A single-shot flame rockets. (Mohammed Shuaib, *Jamiat-e-Islami*)

Right: Afghans waiting at a field clinic set up by doctors from a private voluntary organization inside Afghanistan. (Committee for a Free Afghanistan)

Below left: Decorated Afghan buses – with sheet tin scrollwork and a garish colour scheme – are a primary means of transportation for both guerrillas and civilians inside Afghanistan. Decoration is usually the brightest possible, including religious inscriptions and carpet-like decorative patterns. Some have 12.7mm machine-guns mounted on the roof.

Right: One of the most effective programmes by Western private voluntary organizations has been the training of Afghan para-medics. The Americans lagged behind the Europeans in establishing these, and strong congressional action was required to provide grant support for these efforts, starting in 1985. (US Information Agency)

priority for many of these new leaders, partly mandated by the need to keep people from fleeing to Pakistan or the cities. Especially since 1985, often using aid provided by foreign private voluntary organizations, they have tried to improve agriculture, health care and education. Roads have been built or improved, especially since the increase in air defences limited Soviet helicopter attacks on motor transport.

Resistance Politics

The Resistance parties, headquartered in Pakistan and Iran, pre-date the invasion and are likely to survive the Soviet withdrawal. Attempts to unify the Resistance date back to the 1970s, each proposed unity faltering. The 1980 failure led to the emergence of the competing traditionalist and Islamist unities which existed from 1981 to 1985: the traditionalist one of the parties of Gailani, Mojadiddi, and Mohammedi, and the Islamist one of Rabbani, Khalis, Sayeff, Hekmatyar and three smaller splinter parties. Yet neither unity created a centralized military command or strong political leadership; the Resistance claimed that the Pakistanis – afraid of a possible Lebanon situation if they faced three million exiles with arms and a strong political leader – were blocking greater unity. The Pakistanis claimed that the usual Afghan divisiveness was the cause.

In March 1985, all the major seven parties joined in another alliance, with each party head being spokesman in turn. Similarly, Iran pushed the Shia parties to form their own unity. The Peshawar unity has endured since then, including the formation of a 'provisional government' in February 1988, and the leadership position was strengthened in October 1987, to a *rais* (leader) with a two-year term, abandoned in 1988. The Shia unity, however, fared less well and was inactive by late 1987. In Peshawar the unity and the provisional government have co-existed through 1988.

There is some considerable distrust and resentment towards the Peshawar-based leadership by the guerrillas inside Afghanistan who are actually doing the fighting; support and outside aid being two critical elements often in contention, but almost all guerrillas claim affiliation to one (or more) of the parties because they are the channels through which most outside aid is funnelled by the government of Pakistan, and because the party provides the commanders with political leverage. Beyond this, within the context of the different parties, religious and philosophical divisions have affected the conduct of the war not only in the division between parties, but between individuals and groups inside Afghanistan.

The lack of a central Afghan command hurt strategy, planning and use of resources. But throughout most of the war, such a command headquarters would have been of limited value. It would have been vulnerable to attack or infiltration. The guerrillas had minimal long-range communications capabilities (although Ahmad Shah Massoud's acquisition of a long-range, secure radio network has been a key element in his success).

Even after the signing of the Geneva Accords in 1988, the Resistance still had not evolved the structure of an alternative national government: a constitution or

Above: Resistance radio operator. Secure radio links between Ahmad Shah Massoud, Ismael Khan, and Peshawar contributed to Resistance successes in 1986–8. (Massoud Khalili, *Jamiat-e-Islami*)

Above: Chinese-made 107mm rockets are prepared for action. The availability of these weapons in 1985–8 led the Resistance to emphasize more long-range action on the battlefield, rather than close-range assaults and ambushes, in many areas. (Afghan Media Resource Centre, Peshawar)

fundamental document, shadow ministries, and representation in international bodies. Setting priorities between the parties still remain difficult.

Resistance Strategies

Like the movement itself, the different, often competing, strategies of the Resistance emerged rather than were created. One strategy of concentrating actions along the Pakistani border comes from proximity to ready sources of manpower (in the refugee camps and in the border mountains) and cross-border aid available in Pakistan. Throughout much of the war, these offensive operations have been launched with the hope of taking a major position or town that could serve as a symbolic rallying-point. Kabul regime units in the border area were most vulnerable and Soviet support was limited even at the height of the commitment; at the time of the Soviet withdrawal of May–June 1988, the border areas were where the Resistance could take advantage of opportunities. A competing strategy was that of offensive operations inside Afghanistan. The periphery of Afghanistan was not what the Soviets valued, and so these commanders – such as Abdul Haq – aimed to hit the targets that directly affect the Soviets: cities, roads and airfields. This envisaged its culmination in a possible struggle around Kabul in 1989, combined with winning over people inside the regime. An alternative strategy to these is Ahmad Shah Massoud's consolidation of the north for a protracted conflict. Starting with the

Panjshir Valley at the start of the war, Massoud combined infrastructure building with offensive action. A 13,000-man army is being organized for February 1989. The decentralized nature of the Afghan Resistance has ensured not only that it is difficult to set and keep priorities, but that both main approaches would be carried out, with varying levels of success.

Resistance logistics has shaped all these strategies. Progressive de-population has meant that there are fewer people for the Resistance to draw upon for food and support. Those guerrillas operating in de-populated areas bring food from the cities or from Pakistan, at high cost. The difficulty of moving large amounts of munitions has limited capability for sustained operations throughout the war. Even in 1987–8, for example, there was a shortage of 107mm rockets throughout the Kunar Valley. Soviet interdiction efforts, especially in 1984–6, further compounded the problem. Despite this, the Resistance did not suffer from widespread shortages in 1987–8. There are large weapons caches, especially of small-arms ammunition, throughout Afghanistan. Stingers, however, were given out on an as-needed basis and must be carefully accounted for.

Food inside Afghanistan has been a critical part of Resistance logistics. By 1987, it was thought that 44 per cent of pre-war agricultural capability and 55–70 per cent of output had been lost. While, as early as 1984, the potential existed for an Ethiopia-style famine if the rains were to fail for successive years, this so far has not happened. By 1987–8, there were a number of areas, especially in northern and central Afghanistan, experiencing local shortages, but there was no widespread famine. This is due to the continued flow of food out from cities and from Pakistan, and the fact that about half the population are now refugees, either abroad or internally, primarily in the cities. It does underline the crying need for reconstruction aid if the refugees from Pakistan return home.

The Prophet Mohammed himself was the first refugee in the name of Islam. The Afghan refugees are the key to the future of Afghanistan. Pakistan has handled the difficult refugee problem as well as a developing nation could. Even though there are extensive international aid efforts to

Above: Afghan bread and tea remain the standard food of the Resistance. In 1986–8, the Resistance in eastern Afghanistan became increasingly dependent on food brought in as part of trans-border humanitarian aid. In some cases this could be quite effective – in the 1987–8 Khost battle, guerrillas of Sayeff's group were eating pre-prepared airline-style meals airlifted in from Saudi Arabia. (US Information Agency)

support the refugees, half the total cost of the three to four million refugees fell on Pakistan. The refugee camps have no barbed wire around them, and the Afghans are free to come and go, many travelling throughout Pakistan for work. While there has been some friction with local inhabitants in the North West Frontier Province, where most of the refugee camps are, chiefly over water and pastures, Pathan solidarity has been strong. But by 1987–8 the combination of the costs of the refugee and Soviet-supported terror had made most Pakistanis war-weary.

The 1–1.5 million Afghan refugees in Iran fare less well. Although most live in villages, some are kept in camps behind barbed wire. Some have been conscripted for the Iran–Iraq War. The 100,000 or more in Europe and the United States are significant because they include many of the better educated Afghans, who have been sorely missed both in Peshawar and Afghanistan throughout the course of the war and whose skills will be needed for post-war reconstruction.

The Resistance Groups

Mohaz Milli Islami (National Islamic Front of Afghanistan) of Pir Sayid Ahmad Gailani. Pro-Western in outlook, NIFA is strongest around Kandahar and among the Pathans of the border areas, from Badakhshan down to Ghazni and west to Wardak and Kabul, based on the Pir's status as a Qadiriya Sufi religious leader with followers throughout Pushtu-speaking Afghanistan and with even some influence in the Hazara Jat. Pro-royalist, Gailani is an articulate spokesman.

Jabhe Milli Nejad (National Liberation Front) of Sibghtullah Mojadiddi. Pathan and Naqshbandi Sufic, this group is present in the Jalalabad, Logar, and Kandahar areas, but its Sufic basis for loyalty ensures that supporters will be geographically spread out, without a defined territorial base. While the leadership was anti-royalist pre-war, there is pro-royalist sentiment among the rank and file. Like NIFA, it has had success in attracting former officers, doctors and other educated Afghans, which has given it greater capability, although, as with NIFA, the fusing of Kabuli intellectuals with Pathan tribesmen has often proven difficult. When it pulls together, however, as it sometimes does for NIFA, it can yield an effective fighting force. It is the smallest of the seven Peshawar parties, but Mojadiddi is effective in dealing with both Western and Islamic audiences and leaders.

Harakat-i-Inquilabi-i-Islami (Islamic Revolutionary Movement) of Mohammed Nabi Mohammedi. Numerically large, Harakat represents much of the spirit of traditional Afghanistan. Village-based, its leaders are often local mullahs. It lacks the Sufi background of other traditionalist parties, but its

THE AFGHAN HERITAGE OF GUERRILLA WAR

The Afghans did not have to learn guerrilla warfare in 1978. Louis Dupree's study of Afghan oral traditions revealed that, 'most historical legends deal with inter-tribal or extra-tribal fights' and in a land where mass media had not yet usurped oral tradition as the means of transmitting proper social behaviour, this heritage is a real and living thing.

'. . . The Qazaki "guerrilla" method of warfare is more effective than a pitched battle. . . .There are two prerequisites for this kind of warfare; good horses (mobility) and good archers (fire power). These two can help a small force to defeat a large enemy. . . . When you fight a smaller enemy detachment you should decisively attack with surprise. But if the enemy receives reinforcement and when you encounter a stronger enemy force, avoid decisive engagement and swiftly withdraw only to hit back where the enemy is vulnerable. By this you gain sustainability and the ability to fight a long war of attrition. . . . A war of attrition eventually frustrates the enemy, no matter how strong he may be . . . and that gives a chance of victory to a small force fighting against an invading army.'
–Khushal Khan Khattak, *Dastornama* (17th-century Pushtu epic) – translated by A. A. Jalali.

tive fighting led to an increase in size and influence beginning in about 1985, and they picked up members from a number of more traditional Pathan groups. The party has good relations with Pakistan. It often did well in arms shipments from 1982 to 1986 and, along with the other Hezb party, received the first Stingers in 1986. Khalis was elected *rais* (leader) of the Peshawar seven-party Unity in 1987, being hard-line but willing to consider alternatives in reaching a settlement. It is uncertain to what extent his action reflected the concerns of the Pakistanis and to what extent they were a result of an emerging consensus among the leadership. Khalis certainly had to try and reconcile both requirements. Before the 1988 accord was signed, Khalis gave up the leadership. He is the most anti-royalist of the leadership and personally above corruption.

Jamiat-i-Islami (Islamic Society) of Professor Burhanuddin Rabbani. A moderate Islamist group, Jamiat is numerically large and strongest among the Tadjiks, Uzbeks and Turkomen. Making use of the non-tribal nature of Tadjik society – unlike that of the Pathans – Jamiat has benefited from having the most effective regional commanders in Dari-speaking areas. Anti-royalist, but not anti-Western in outlook, Jamiat has been attacked by more extreme fundamentalists, with Khalis being its closest ally. Jamiat has attracted Pathan supporters in Kabul province, the Kunar Valley, Paktia and the Kandahar area. Active throughout Dari-speaking Afghanistan; Herat, Mazar-e-Sharif, Badakshan, Takhar, Parwan and Kapisa provinces all have Jamiat strongholds.

authority also remains religious rather than territorial or political. Strongest among Pathans, with widespread support, especially in the Helmand Valley, Ghazni, Wardak, Koh-i-Safi, Badakshan and Kunar, it also had support among the Uzbeks and Turkomen of the north in the first three years of the war, although these later tended to support Jamiat. Two breakaway factions, mainly concentrated in the north, associated themselves with the Islamist unity (and, in some cases, with Iran starting in 1987) while Mohammedi was associated with the traditionalist unity.

Hezbi-i-Islami (Islamic Party) of Younis Khalis. Khalis is a moderate Islamist, with his strongest support among Pathans. He was formerly associated with the other Hezb party. It is the most powerful party in Nangrahar, including the Kunar Valley, and this gives him a strong base that the other six parties cannot match in Pushtu-speaking Afghanistan. Kabul and Paktika provinces have a strong Khalis presence. Khalis was the only Pakistan-based leader who regularly fought inside Afghanistan. Originally relatively small, this party's hard and effec-

Ittehad-e-Islami (Islamic Alliance) of Professor Abdul Rasoul Sayeff. A 1980 escapee from Kabul, Sayeff was brought in to head the proposed 1980 all-party unity due largely to his access to money and weapons through his links to Muslim Brotherhood and Wahabi groups in the Arab world. He ended up forming his own party to which he attracted many guerrillas in 1982–4. Since then, because of his lack of a firm, traditional base of authority, except in parts of his native Paghman, many have left with their arms. He also has some influence in Kabul, Nangrahar, Paktika and Paktia and increased links with Jamiat in mid-1988. His fighting men are well armed and equipped, though sometimes derided as 'Gucci guerrillas'.

Hezb-i-Islami (Islamic Party) of Gulbuddin Hekmatyar. The most controversial Peshawar-based leader, Hekmatyar was one of the first to take up *jihad* and so had many adherents; an engineering student, he fled to Pakistan in 1974 and started armed resistance against the Daoud regime. Ruthless in tactics and genuinely revolutionary and Islamist in orientation, Hekmatyar's forces under Jaglan Niazi blocked the supply routes to the Panjshir in 1984, attacked Panjshiri forces in 1981, and fought against Massoud's efforts to consolidate the north in 1987–8. Almost every report of inter-Afghan fighting involves them. Hekmatyar has considerable outside support, from Pakistan and Arab nations. Less tied to traditional Afghan values than any other party, and mainly Pathan, the party is widespread although without individual strong commanders. Strongholds include, in the north: in Laghman, Ghorband, and Baghlan; in the Kunar, Paktia and Logar; and in the south, in Helmand, Ghazni and among the Aimaq. However, its influence is apparently declining, with serious internal divisions becoming apparent by 1987–8. Hekmatyar was re-elected head of his party in 1987, and in 1988 he succeeded Khalis as head of the Peshawar-based Resistance leadership. The outlook of both the leadership and many of those in the field (people who would be in WAD if they were fighting for the quisling regime tend to gravitate to Hekmatyar if they are fighting for the Resistance) and their taste for power has given rise to fears about a Hekmatyar move on Kabul, perhaps with a pre-existing deal with PDPA elements. His lack of a traditional base means that he is dependent on outside support and good relations with Pakistan. The Pakistanis certainly supported him pre-1978 and during the course of the war they have usually given his group priority in arms shipments. The late President Zia was a strong supporter of Hekmatyar, as was the Chief of Staff. Despite suspicions from other Afghans that he has his own agenda, and has been limiting his operations against the Soviets since mid-1987 to prepare for power struggles, Hekmatyar continues to command respect.

Shia Afghanistan and the Iranian Connection

Because of the Sunni orientation of the seven major Peshawar-based parties, Afghanistan's Shia minority has tended to look to alternate leadership. This has led to a number of separate Shia parties being formed, which, like the Sunni parties, did not form a real unity until 1985, but before then have engaged in much more bitter inter-group hostility than even their Sunni counterparts.

The Hazara Jat has been a separate war within a war. Set apart from their fellow Afghans by their Mongol features, Shia Islam, and mountain-ringed homeland, Hazaras were the nearest thing Afghanistan had to the dispossessed. Although one of the senior PDPA leaders – Sultan Ali Keshtmand – is a Hazara, the majority are violently anti-Communist. Kabul-based Hazaras were instrumental in 'The Night of Allah Akbar'. Early in the war, the Kabul regime garrisons in the Hazara Jat were either taken or joined the Resistance, except for a handful that paid high tributes to remain intact until abandoned in 1988. Shura-i-Inquilabi (Revolutionary Council) under Doctor Sayid Ahmad Beheshti, was in 1979–85 the 'official' government of the Hazara Jat, comprising a broad coalition of different Hazara groups. It set up a sophisticated autonomous government, with 'regular' armed forces and taxation. Soon after the invasion, the Hazara Jat was in large part free of Communist forces and was under the Shura party government.

By 1982, radical Shia Islam started to mount a strong challenge to Shura authority. Sazmar-i-Nasr (Organization for Victory), the Iranian-funded revolutionary opposition in the Hazara Jat, moved against the Shura in that year. Sepah, an allied party, had a similar background. The Pasadran (Revolutionary Guards), mainly in the Hazara Jat, linked to its Iranian equivalents, was also opposed to the Shura, a position compounded by extensive Communist infiltration, both by the PDPA and the Iranian Tudeh. The pro-Iranian revolutionary Hezbollah party also has a small following inside Afghanistan.

In 1980–6, most of the limited Iranian aid and support – much less than Pakistan – for the Resistance was directed to Shia groups, especially Nasr, Sepah and the Pasadran. By 1984, two-thirds of the Hazara Jat was under the authority of the radical parties. The increased, Iranian-funded activities of Nsar, Sepah, the Padsaran and other more radical groups in the Hazara Jat by 1985 gave them the upper hand. Once all these parties had joined in the Shia unity in 1985, combined Hazara forces were able to strike outside the Hazara Jat and to defeat Kabul regime efforts at the end of that year to re-establish a presence in the Hazara Jat. In 1987, however, changes in the Iranian Government contributed to a break between the Shia resistance and Iran. Even groups such as the Padsaran were reluctant to do Tehran's bidding. Instead Iran was working more closely with

some of the smaller Sunni groups, such as Mansur's Harakat faction.

The Harakat-i-Islami (Islamic Party) of Sheikh Assef Mohseni, however, is found throughout the Shia population (Mohseni is from Kandahar) rather than limited to the Hazaras. It is an opponent of the radical Shia-backed parties and devoted to the anti-Soviet war, which some other Shia parties largely ignore. It has some of the most effective guerrillas in and around Kabul. The party lost power after the formation of the 1985 Shia unity.

The different Sunni groups have had varying success in their relations with Iran. Jamiat, whose guerrillas operate near the Iranian border near Herat, have moved to improve relations. By 1985–7, Iran apparently permitted supplies to go to Sunni groups in western Afghanistan, although it did not contribute to the aid flow. In return, the Afghans agreed to accept pro-Iranian groups inside their territory, and Iran has funded a large-scale outreach effort towards

Below: Nicknamed 'BM-1' by the Resistance, a Chinese-made single-tube 107mm rocket-launcher is, together with the 82mm mortar, the most common Resistance indirect fire weapon. When launch tubes are not available, the Resistance will simply place a rocket on a wood bipod or on some rocks, point in the direction of the enemy, and fire. (Afghan Media Resource Centre, Peshawar)

the Dari-speaking Sunni population inside Afghanistan.

Resistance on the Left

The overall Islamic orientation of the Resistance has meant that there has never been a significant left-wing component to the anti-Soviet war. Afghan Millat was an indigenous anti-Soviet national socialist party under Mohammed Amin Wakman. It was a follow-on of the 1960s Social Democratic Party, but it splintered in the late 1970s and, while it fielded a few resistance groups after the invasion, by 1983 it had collapsed. Other left-wing Resistance groups included Shola-i-Javaid (Eternal Flame), a small Kabul-based Maoist group which collapsed by 1981. SAMA was an offshoot of Shola. While its 'independent Marxist' adherents were very few, it was the

only Resistance Party to emphasize assassinations. It had collapsed by 1982–3. The Settim-e-Melli, another tiny left-wing Resistance group, joined the Kabul regime about the same time.

Resistance Leaders

The commanders of the Afghan Resistance range from the pre-eminent – Ahmad Shah Massoud is certainly that – to natural guerrilla leaders – Abdul Haq is certainly that – to those with more limited areas of operations or battlefield success. Not all the commanders have been effective throughout the war; many only earned their status after many years and many casualties. Other commanders, once they had gained a reputation, have rested on their laurels and used this 'renown' to secure more support from Peshawar and overseas while not doing much fighting. There are about 900 significant commanders inside Afghanistan. A few of the better-known ones include:

Ahmad Shah Massoud. Tadjik, Jamiat. This most famous Afghan guerrilla has moved beyond his native Panjshir Valley, where he has organized and led forces that the Soviets have not defeated in nine offensives, to organize the entire north of Afghanistan. His 1983–4 ceasefire was controversial, but Massoud's influence is increasing throughout north Afghanistan. He has formed the Supervisory Council of the North to co-ordinate different groups. A student of guerrilla strategy, his effective political and civil infrastructure-building is the best in Afghanistan. He has not left the country since 1975, and may have the potential to be a national leader, but it is uncertain whether Pushtu-speaking Afghanistan would accept him. His achievement in the north, however, suggests that it is possible he may be able to play a national role.

Hadji-Abdul Haq. Pathan, Hezb (Khalis), ex-student. Operating around Kabul, he is the most effective single Pathan Resistance leader. Abdul Haq was a comrade of Abdul Halim until he was killed in action in 1982, when Haq emerged as the most significant commander around Kabul. In 1985, however, increasing Soviet pressure had forced

Below: Abdul Haq, a keen guerrilla tactician as well as an accomplished Resistance diplomat – he has met both Thatcher and Reagan. He learned English from journalists and can actually speak it intelligibly. Highly intelligent and quick-witted, but with limited formal education (he was arrested while in high school for his Islamist activities), he will be a significant man in war or peace. (David C. Isby)

Abdul Haq to modify his operations around Kabul. Urban guerrilla operations become more difficult, and de-population affected resistance throughout Kabul Province. Wounded many times, his forces use SA-7s and Chinese-made 107mm rocket-launchers with good effect. Keenly intelligent, hard fighting, perhaps the finest guerrilla offensive tactician and a first-class fighting man, but with an excellent grasp of international and Resistance politics as well.

Sayid Jaglan. Hazara. Shura. An ex-major in the Kabul regime, he is now Commander of *Shura* forces. He scored several victories in 1979–80, but since then, he has often been embroiled in the fighting in the Hazara Jat between the Shia parties. In late 1985, Hazara guerrillas scored a number of victories against Kabul regime forces near Bamiyan (liberated June 1988) and Ghazni.

Zabioullah. Tadjik. Jamiat. An ex-religious teacher he was the chief commander of Resistance around Mazar-e-Sharif until killed in action during December 1984 and replaced by Mohammed Alim. Alim's personal influence was not as substantial as Zabioullah's, and increased Soviet pressure in the Mazar area led to Ahmad Shah Massoud assuming a stronger role in the area from 1985.

Ismael Khan. Tadjik. Jamiat. Ismael Khan, then a major in the Kabul regime army, joined the Resistance at Herat in 1979. Originally a local commander, by 1985–7 he had emerged as not only the main Resistance commander around Herat, but throughout the west, emulating Massoud's regional approach. He called his first regional Council in Ghowr in the summer of 1987. His main tactical subordinate is Alluladin Khan, also ex-military.

Shabioullah. Pathan. Harakat. A mullah, killed in action, April 1985, he had strong guerrilla forces in the Koh-i-safi area northeast of Kabul.

Qari Tadj Mohammed. Pathan. Harakat. An ex-lawyer and guerrilla leader in the Ghazni area. Hard-fighting, he has eliminated much of the PDPA infrastructure and cadre in his area.

Jalulladin Haqani Pathan. Hezbi (Khalis). Another mullah, he emerged in 1985 as the foremost guerrilla leader in south Paktia and Paktika provinces. Haqani, was the main

leader involved in the 1985 siege of Khost and the 1985, 1986 and 1987–8 Paktia offensives. His co-operation with other groups has greatly increased since 1985. Universally respected as a fighter, he is slow and deliberate but well-considered in his decision-making. Leader of the Zadron tribe of the Pathans.

Mullah Nassim Akhundzade. Pathan. Harakat. Helmand area's chief commander, he works closely with local religious leadership (all from same *madrassa*).

Mohammed Shah. Pathan. Harakat. A mullah and regional commander in the Farah area.

Sher Ahmad Kandahari. Pathan. Harakat. Also a mullah he was a commander in Nangrahar Province, Shinwar district, until killed in action during 1986.

Mohammed Amin Wardak. Pathan. NIFA. An ex-Ministry of Tourism official, he became a local commander in Wardak Province. He is known for his effective development and civic action programmes and has devoted a great deal of time to international relations, travelling widely, as well as the civil administration of his area of Wardak Province. In co-operation with other commanders, he has been, in 1986, striking targets away from his home area.

Far left, top: 'Qari Baba' is the nickname of Qari Tadj Mohammed (left). A fierce and merciless fighter even by Pathan standards, he earned the title of *Qari* by committing the Koran to memory. A lawyer pre-war, like the present author (who would not like to have him for an opponent on the battlefield or in the courtroom). (David C. Isby)

Far left, bottom: Amin Wardak, the well-known Resistance leader. Amin was one of the first to try and create an alternative government, providing services such as education, medicine – even a postal service. Unlike Ahmad Shah Massoud, however, Amin's aims are local rather than regional. (David C. Isby)

Near left, top: Abdul Rahim Wardak, guerrilla commander of the National Islamic Front of Afghanistan. Peshawar-based, Rahim was a colonel in the Afghan Army before the war. He is an effective planner, making use of a broad and deep knowledge of military history. (David C. Isby)

Left: Ramatullah Safi had led guerrillas in combat in Paktia and Kunar. A former colonel in the Royal Afghan Army, he is a charismatic leader and a thoughtful soldier who has sought to spread training throughout the Resistance. (David C. Isby)

Engineer Bashir. Pathan. Hezb (Hekmatyar). A major commander in Badakshan and north, he co-exists uneasily with Massoud.

Mohammed Anwar. Pathan. Jamiat. An ex-teacher and athlete, he is a local commander in the Jagdalak area, Kabul province. He also operated in Paktia in 1986–7 as his area of operations was de-populated. A keen defensive tactician.

Abdul Rahim Wardak. Pathan. NIFA. An ex-colonel with the Kabul regime, he is now Peshawar-based and has led combat operations throughout the border areas and Kabul.

Ramatullah Safi. Pathan. NIFA. An ex-colonel with the Royal Afghan Army, he too is Peshawar-based today; noted for training as well as combat in Paktia (attacked Khost airfield during 1986 Zhawar fighting) and Kunar (blocked a Soviet relief column, 1987).

Ghulam Mohammed Aryanpur. Tajik. Jamiat. An ex-religious teacher, he is the senior Jamiat commander in Badakshan, working closely with Massoud in the Council of the North.

Hadji Mohammed Anwar. Pathan. Independent. An ex-DRA pilot, he operates in Farah.

Hadji Mohammed Shah. Pathan. Harakat. A mullah who is also the major commander in Farah. He co-operates with Ismael Khan.

Hadji Abdul Kadir. Pathan. *Hezb* (Khalis). The brother of Abdul Haq, he is a commander in Nangrahar Province.

Hadji Abdul Latif. Pathan. NIFA. Known as 'The Lion of Kandahar', he is one of the major commanders in the Kandahar area.

Lala Malang. Pathan. Harakat. A major commander in the Kandahar area.

Nakib Akhund. Pathan. Jamiat. A mullah and now their major commander, Kandahar area.

Mahmoud Khan. Tadjik. Jamiat. A lawyer; the subordinate of Massoud, he commands operations in the Panjshir itself while Massoud looks to regional issues.

Faiz Mohammed. Pathan. Hezb (Hekmatyar). An Engineer, he is the most senior of Hekmatyar's commanders in Paktia.

Hashmat Mojadiddi. Jabha. Pathan. A medical doctor and commander in Nangrahar Province. He is related to the leadership family in Peshawar.

Assadullah Falah. Jabha. Pathan. Another ex-officer now a commander in Logar Province.

Anwar and Shams. Hazara. Harakat (Mohseni). Two of the most effective Resistance leaders in the Kabul area, with many supporters among the local Shia population.

Resistance Tactics

I n many places, early war tactics followed traditional modes of fighting. In 1979 in Paktia, for example, tribal forces (*lashkars*) were formed and pitched battles were successfully fought against DRA forces. But such large-scale, relatively spontaneous, actions – the rural counterpart of the urban risings seen in Herat, Kandahar and Kabul in 1979–80 – were disastrous in the face of Soviet firepower. With the Soviets in place in the cities, the Resistance was, starting in 1980, basically one of thousands of autonomous fronts (*jabhas*), each with its own village and stronghold.

Slowly, the Afghans have evolved organizations looking beyond these local commands, embracing a valley, a province, or, in the case of Ahmad Shah Massoud, several provinces. This allows a broader scope for operations, both military and political. Even in areas where there is no one commander or party predominating, such as around Kandahar, councils and command procedures have evolved to allow combined operations.

AHMAD SHAH MASSOUD: RESISTANCE STRATEGY

'In general, guerrilla or revolutionary wars have three stages. We have four: to set our objectives, to develop a strategic offence, and general preparation. We are now (1987) in the second step of this ten-year process. (While he has drawn on Mao's writing) 'there is no single person I could say has influenced me or impressed me that much'.

Right: The War in the North, 1986–8. This diagram shows a typical DRA garrison. It is in a valley, along a road which is blocking the Afghans moving between two adjacent valleys. It is built around an old fort, with a tower (now armed with a heavy machine-gun). The garrison has three dug-in T-34-85 tanks, one 76.2mm field gun, and a battery of four mortars plus about 200 troops, DRA regulars, militia, and WAD. It is surrounded by dense minefields and a double belt of barbed wire. In the past, all the local Resistance would do was harass such a garrison. Ahmad Shah Massoud, however, would, through thorough reconnais-sance, determine the gaps in the minefields and the location of the heavy weapons. Then he would position blocking forces and put down mines between the garrison and potential reinforcements. 107mm rocket-launchers and 82mm mortars would be brought up close to the garrisons. After a brief but intense barrage, the Central Forces and the local *majahideen* would storm through the gaps in the minefields.

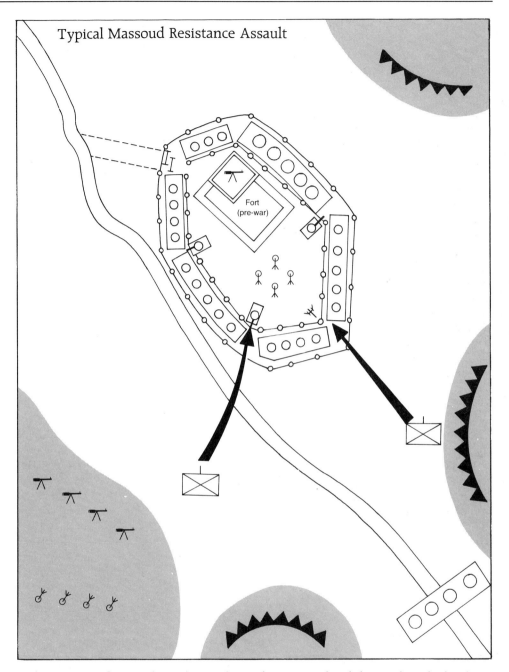

Typical Massoud Resistance Assault

Fort (pre-war)

The transition from traditional to modern guerrilla came slowly, even in the Panjshir Valley. Massoud (who started by doing all his military training himself) set up training programmes for his troops and, starting in 1983, dispatched mobile training teams throughout the north. Other groups have since followed suit and set up training camps in the border areas. But as late as 1984, a Jamiat official estimated that only 5–10 per cent of the guerrillas' manpower has

been trained and the rest have had to learn how to fight by surviving in battle. By 1987–8, the percentage was several times that, especially in the east. The level of training remains low, and usually does not proceed above what Western armies would consider individual soldier, weapons crew, or squad or section level tactics.

Better training of the leaders and indivi-dual Afghans has contributed to the improvement of the Resistance. 'More

weapons without more training means only more martyrs,' said Mohammed Amin Wardak in 1984. Yet the absence of military rear area support for the guerrillas means that training is limited. While, in some groups, ex-soldiers have trained their comrades, for much of the war even the military skills and knowledge available to the Resistance was not fully used. There certainly has been a need for training in all areas of military skills; for while the Afghans like to consider themselves natural shots, their overall standard of marksmanship is actually rather low.

What has also improved the effectiveness of the Resistance has been the harsh Darwinism of the battlefield. Those leaders with more courage than sense are already long dead and those without determination are in exile. Those who proved radical

(except Hekmatyar) or tyrannical have largely been overthrown. This process is most pronounced in areas where there has been a great deal of fighting. For example, the Soviets made their first offensive into the Helmand Valley in 1985. The local Afghans, without combat experience, suffered heavy casualties, because they practised the old ways of raiding and limited warfare.

Ambushes are the standard method of both offensive and defensive combat. Afghans will, if forced, fight a defensive battle, around a village or other objective, but generally prefer to use ambush tactics. Ambushes are used to interdict supply convoys more often than blocking roads. The Resistance ability to close roads would probably prevent a PDPA regime from fighting on long after the Soviets have left.

Ahmad Shah Massoud has shown more success in taking garrisons. Techniques developed in the Panjshir in 1985 have been applied in battles throughout the north from 1986–8. But Massoud's approach requires painstaking reconnaissance and planning, and is done in combination with political and development work in the area of each attack. Like most effective tactics in a guerrilla war, it is not purely military. Massoud spent the year 1987 concentrating on building a resistance organization which he believes will last as long as there is any Soviet presence. Massoud is not aiming for a quick victory, but rather to prevail over the long haul of protracted guerrilla warfare. To achieve this, Massoud has worked with fighting men from different parties as an integral part of his political strategy. He is creating an alternative to the discredited Kabul government in the best traditions of wars of national liberation.

Throughout the war, but especially since 1984–5, the increased availability of long-range weapons – 82mm mortars and 107mm and 122mm rockets – has led to another form of offensive action. On occasion, this has resulted in success, such as the attacks on the PDPA anniversary celebrations in 1985 and on munitions storage depots at Kargha and Bagram in 1986, and Kalagay in 1988, but often it is not repeated, systematic or sustained, simply mere harassment. In 1987, the Resistance fielded increased

numbers of Chinese-made 107mm and 122mm rocket-launchers which have become a critical battlefield weapon. In 1986–7 the Resistance relied on them to counter Communist offensives with long-range fire as well as to apply this firepower offensively. In 1988 rocket attacks against Kabul, Jalalabad and other cities increased.

The 1986–8 period also saw more RPG–7s (although ammunition supply remains a problem) and anti-tank mines. The Resistance's lack of minefield breaching equipment and training has kept many garrisons from falling and may become more significant if 1989 brings fighting around the Kabul defences. While some groups have improvised Bangalore torpedoes and grappling hooks, the US supply of portable rocket-propelled mine-clearing line charges in 1988 was the first specialized equipment to reach the Resistance but most of these were destroyed in the ammunition dump explosion.

The only real city in Afghanistan is Kabul. The potential exists to turn Kabul into a reasonable facsimile of Beirut. The Afghans,

however, have not been able to exploit this potential, despite the obvious anti-Soviet sentiment in the capital, demonstrated as early as 'the Night of Allah Akbar' in 1980. Until 1985, there were significant numbers of Afghans operating as urban guerrillas. Mainly in night-time raids, commanders such as Abdul Haq, Shams and those of the SAMA and other splinter organizations were able to stage ambushes and bombings throughout the city, as well as attacking military positions and headquarters. But the regime and the Soviets poured more resources into the Kabul defences which included, it is estimated, more than 20,000 regime troops by 1987. In 1987, the major guerrilla commanders had to restrict themselves to car-bombs and attacks emphasizing longer-ranged weapons. The inability to mobilize the people within the Kabul perimeter actively to join the Resistance is mitigated by the fact that many of them send money and information out to the Resistance.

The cities, always important, became more so throughout the war as their

Right: An Afghan checks his RPD light machine-gun while resting on the wreck of an Mi-17 Hip-H helicopter, Jadji, June 1987. If the Russians do fully withdraw, the Kabul regime will not have had time to train large numbers of helicopter pilots to replace losses such as this one, or to compensate for the absence of the Soviets. (Afghan Media Resource Centre, Peshawar)

Left: The RPG-7 remains, along with mines, the Resistance's main anti-tank weapon. (Massoud Khalili, *Jamiat-e-Islami*)

populations increased with internal refugees and those on the government payroll, either directly or indirectly (such as those working on regime-sponsored construction). This created a population that might be considered potential supporters – out of war-weariness, if nothing else – for a peace acceptable to Moscow.

In Herat and Kandahar, Communist control has been limited throughout the war. Afghans operate between the city and the airfield, in the suburbs, and can even carry arms openly in the bazaar. However, in 1987 the Soviets responded by desolating great areas of both cities, which have already suffered substantial de-population in the close-in areas. In Mazar-e-Sharif and Jalalabad, however, there is a greater degree of control and security, and Resistance attacks tend to be made with long-range weapons. These cities were, within their perimeters, relatively secure in 1987–8.

The 1987 fighting demonstrated that although the Afghans may not have come to grips with guerrilla war strategy and may not be able to use modern weaponry in the most effective way, they have a good grasp of basic guerrilla tactics. Resistance offensive action in 1987 has been against cities, airfields, supply routes and forts and garrisons. The Resistance interdiction efforts were often not well directed or sustained, despite the Stingers used against attack helicopters on convoy escort duty. Despite this, a number of major road closings took place.

Regional concentration of fighting men and commanders allows the Resistance to deploy more powerful forces and Commanders who have gained a good reputation for fighting elsewhere will usually be welcomed by other Afghans, especially if they have the Stingers.

Weapons

Afghan rifles originally included percussion jezails and Martini-Henrys captured at Maiwand in 1880 (Afghans invariably assign this provenance to any Martini-Henry, but most were smuggled in at the turn of the century). The two most common weapons are .303in Lee Enfields in various versions and, the weapon that has replaced it since 1983–4, a wide range of 7.62mm Kalashnikov assault rifles. These include standard AK-47s and AKMs and their folding stock versions. The Chinese (most common), Romanian and Egyptian versions have been supplied as part of outside aid to the Resistance.

The first crop of Kalashnikovs came with the Kabul regime desertions of 1979–80 and they have since been increased by capture and outside aid. The Soviet 5.45mm AK-74, and the folding stock AKS-74 AKSU are known as the 'Kallikov' by the *mujahideen*. They are obtained only by capture. Lee Enfields were common pre-war, and many were included in outside aid during the first years of the war. In many groups, the older guerrillas use the Lee Enfields for long-range fire, the younger men the Kalashnikovs at close range. By 1987, however, Lee Enfields

Left: Chinese-built versions of the 7.62mm RPD light machine-gun are in standard use by the Resistance. These weapons became more numerous after 1984, which coincided with a general raising of Resistance tactical skills to include an awareness of what Western armies would consider squad-level tactics. Before this, the idea that if, say, there were thirty fighting men, they should be divided into three groups of ten with someone in charge of each group and a single commander over all three groups did not occur to many *mujaheds*. (David C. Isby)

Right: Afghan guerrilla with a captured 80mm RPG-22 disposable single-shot anti-tank rocket-launcher. These weapons, like the 66mm RPG-18, have detailed instructions for use in Russian on the side of the tube so, with translation, the Resistance have been able to fire captured examples. (*Jamiat-e-Islami*, Afghanistan)

were rare, especially in eastern Afghanistan, due to the influx of Kalashnikovs.

SKS 7.62mm rifles (Soviet and Chinese made) are used in smaller numbers. In the first years of the war, M-1891 Moisin-Nagant 7.62mm rifles (supplied to Afghanistan at Lenin's order in 1920) were still to be seen. 7.62mm G3 (ex-Iranian) rifles are sometimes encountered and like East German-made Kalashnikovs and Soviet 5.45mm weapons, they are a status symbol.

A variety of light machine-guns is used, and the 7.62mm RPD (nicknamed 'Sadtaka', often Chinese-made versions) and RPK are most common, along with 7.62mm SGMs and PKMs and older Czech-made ZB 36s. RPG-7 anti-tank grenade-launchers (Soviet and Chinese made) are used, together with 75mm and 82mm recoilless anti-tank guns (Chinese, Soviet and Czech) and a range of anti-tank mines, both Soviet and Western designs. These have been supplied in large quantities: the Soviets claim to have removed 4,500 from the road to Khost in January 1988. By early 1988, there were reports that the Resistance had received 160 European-designed Milan anti-tank guided missile-launchers, along with training for gunners. These proved effective in action throughout 1988.

Soviet-designed DShKM 12.7mm and 14.5mm KPV heavy machine-guns, 'Dashika' and 'Zigroiat' respectively to the Afghans, are used against both aircraft and ground targets. Since 1982 more weapons, especially Chinese-made versions, have become

common: the Panjshir Valley was defended by thirteen heavy machine-guns in 1982 and by 200 to 250 two years later. Not only did numbers improve, but so did the use made of them. The Afghans knew nothing of field fortifications and improved gun positions in the early years of the war, but by 1984 had started to dig in earnest throughout much of Afghanistan. Since 1985, a limited number (30 or less) of 20mm Oerlikon-designed light AA guns have been used, especially in the Kunar valley and in Paktia. Chinese-made versions of the Soviet ZU-23 twin 23mm cannon are also used.

Man-portable heat-seeking SA-7 *Grail* surface-to-air missiles have been in use since 1980: the Kabul regime army had SA-7s pre-war. Capture, cash purchases on the world arms market (especially from the PLO as they left Beirut in 1982), and a limited aid flow have provided additional weapons. But SA-7s were never able to make the Soviets less willing to use their airpower offensively; as the Stinger and Blowpipe SAMs were to do in September 1986, they merely forced them to attack less accurately from higher altitude and use evasive action and counter-measures. The most significant single, weapons system supplied to the Resistance is the Stinger surface-to-air missile. The first

Above: A plastic anti-tank mine in standard Resistance service. Though not made in Italy, the Soviets know them as 'Italian mines'. While mine warfare was not unknown to the Pathans pre-war – those on the other side of the Durand Line were using dud shells and bombs as mines against the British in the 1930s – the Resistance lacked training in effective mine warfare. This was remedied, as the aid flow increased, by sheer weight of numbers, so much so that many guerrillas took to scooping the explosive out of mines to fuel their stoves. (David C. Isby)

STINGERS – THE IMPACT

'What turned this whole thing around was the provision of the Stingers. It's a pity and scandalous that we didn't do this earlier in the war.' – US Senator Gordon Humphrey (Republican of New Hampshire, one of the Congressional architects of US policy in 1984–8).

'There are only two things Afghans must have: the Koran and Stingers.' – Ahmad Shah Massoud.

'The Soviets don't use their helicopter gunships very much any more. They are now mainly used for operations at night rather than on the battlefield.' – Mohammed Amin Wardak, 1987.

'Jet flights have been reduced by 50 per cent this year.' – Jalulladin Haqani, 1987.

'Only a handful of jets fly into the valley every day at very high altitude to drop a few bombs before leaving the area as soon as possible, apparently afraid of the *mujahideen*'s sophisticated anti-aircraft weapons. Helicopters have become a rare sight.' – Floris Van Stratten, Hajibad, Kunar, 6 July 1987.

'(Stingers) . . . created additional difficulties for Afghan Army and Soviet troops. This led to additional casualties among Afghan and Soviet troops and the air force.' – Soviet deputy Foreign Ministry spokesman, Boris Pyadyshev, 16 July 1987.

'Your (American) missiles and your women, they are both very dangerous.' – sexist utterance by Soviet journalist, Khost, Paktia province, January 1988.

Right: The 14.5mm ZPU-1 and ZGU-1, nicknamed 'Ziqrioat' in both its Chinese- and Soviet-built versions, is a standard Resistance air defence weapon. The Soviet and Kabul regime forces have used similar versions in static defensive positions. A powerful weapon, it can demolish all but the strongest wall and, with armour-piercing ammunition, penetrate the 7mm titanium belly armour of a Hind. (David C. Isby)

of these US-made weapons arrived in 1986 and, according to Press reports, Resistance gunners were hand-picked and trained by foreign advisers, outside Afghanistan. Routine Soviet anti-SA-7 counter-measures had little effect against the Stingers and Blowpipes. The Stinger uses an improved version of the SA-7's heat-seeking guidance. The Blowpipe, though less accurate and requiring better gunner training, is visually guided and relatively immune to counter-measures. The initial supply of Stingers was limited to only 600 missiles; another 300 or so followed soon afterwards. Strict restric-

tions were placed on their use to reduce the chance of diversion of weapons to non-Resistance sources and to maintain the security of the resupply. Despite this, a limited number was seized by, or sold to, Iranian Revolutionary Guards, and a few were turned over to the Soviets; others have been captured in battle.

The most common indirect fire weapon is still the Soviet M-1937 82mm mortar, in both its Soviet- and Chinese-made versions. Simple and robust, it is limited by its 3km range. It is supplemented by smaller numbers of Chinese-designed 60mm

Left: Until overshadowed by the Stinger and the Blowpipe, the Soviet SA-7 Grail was the Resistance's only surface-to-air missile. In addition to those arriving through arms aid channels, others were purchased by the Resistance in Beirut in 1981–2 or from elsewhere in the Middle East. It is not a 'soldier-proof' weapon and is much more difficult to use effectively than the more sophisticated Stinger. (Afghan Media Resource Centre, Peshawar)

Left: The 'Dashika', the 12.7mm DShKM heavy machine-gun – here positioned in front of a bombed-out house near Herat – remains, with both Soviet- and Chinese-built versions, the standard Resistance air defence weapon. Such emplacements, especially in the ruins of houses sited on high ground, are common throughout Afghanistan. Most guerrilla strongholds are surrounded by several such machine-gun positions. Where ruins are not available, the machine-guns will be set up in rocks. (Massoud Khalili, *Jamiat-e-Islami*)

mortars. The longer-ranged (8km) Chinese-designed 107mm rockets are fired from 12-tube launchers, single-tube launchers, or even from rocks and improvised mounts. In 1986–8, single-tube Soviet-designed and multi-tube Egyptian-designed 122mm rocket-launchers were being used against the Kabul defences and in late 1987, light 120mm mortars (reportedly Spanish-made) with their attendant hand-held fire control computers were in action against Soviet garrisons. However, as late as 1987, the complexities of indirect fire, even with relatively simple weapons, remained above the heads of even some of the better Afghan commanders.

The Resistance has captured a considerable amount of armour and artillery from the Kabul regime's army, or had it presented to them by ralliers but use is limited by shortages of trained personnel, enemy command of the air, and the shortage of fuel and ammunition, Resistance armour and artillery has been used in operations in the provinces bordering Pakistan: T-54 and T-55 main battle tanks, BMP-1 infantry fighting vehicles, BTR-60PB and BTR-152 armoured personnel carriers, D-30 and M-30 122mm howitzers and M-1942 76.2mm mountain guns, all Soviet made.

Outside Aid

The Soviet claims of outside aid for the Resistance appear to date from before its provision. Their broadcasts at the time of the invasion included claims about the activities of foreign agents who were responsible for the war in Afghanistan. Without ever producing these individuals (even the author of this book was alleged to be one), the Soviets reiterated this propaganda for domestic consumption for a number of years.

Outside aid falls into a much broader category than simply the provision of munitions for the Resistance. It has consisted of three basic tracks: economic sanctions, diplomatic activity and aid – military and humanitarian – targeted inside Afghanistan.

The economic sanctions on the Soviet Union did not, for the most part, endure past the mid-1980s. They had also been subsumed into those following the imposition of martial law in Poland. Few barriers remained after the improvement in east-west relations in 1987. Economic sanctions on the Kabul regime were more

Right: Resistance motor transport uses a variety of civil vehicles available in Pakistan. The flag (that of NIFA) serves as a recognition signal to sentries. (David C. Isby)

limited, and it retained even its US 'Most Favoured Nation' status until Congressional pressure forced its removal in 1985.

Diplomatic activity has been more mixed. The initial flurry of anti-Soviet action was replaced, despite the increasing votes in the UN General Assembly, with what appeared to be a perception that the Soviets had occupied Afghanistan and its pacification would soon be a *fait accompli*. The Resistance's own diplomatic weakness – it could not agree as to who would serve as all-party representatives or what its policies should be – contributed to the lack of decisive diplomatic action. But over the years, the continued fighting inside Afghanistan eventually challenged these assumptions. In the United States, under pressure from Congress, Afghanistan began to be seen as a more significant issue. This was reflected, for example, in its higher status on the agenda at the 1987 Washington Summit compared to the 1985 Geneva Summit.

While the Pakistanis had already supplied some arms and training as early as the mid-1970s, they, along with the Afghans' foreign supporters – USA, Egypt, Saudi Arabia, China, the Gulf States, and others – only started a significant arms flow in 1980. There was not a lot of thought and organization to the early flow: much of the hardware was outdated; and there was little, if any, provision for training. After less than a year of this chaotic activity, the Pakistanis took steps to regularize and rationalize the flow, and then took full control. While the agencies and individuals involved changed during the course of the war, the ultimate form of Pakistani oversight and control had been set up by late 1982, and the policy of deniability – officially, there are no arms coming in for the Resistance – has been maintained throughout the war.

As we have seen, by 1986–7, most of the weapons coming in to the Resistance were Chinese-made, with Egyptian, Soviet, and eastern bloc equipment also in the pipeline. Paying for them were, among others, the United States, Saudi Arabia, and China. While all these forms of assistance are channelled through the government of Pakistan, some aid (especially Arab programmes of non-governmental groups) is targeted directly to the Resistance itself. By 1988, the total annual outside financial aid to the Resistance was about one billion dollars a year, with the United States providing the largest amount, followed by the Saudis and the Chinese.

The total amount of US arms aid throughout the war has been about two billion dollars, but it was only after Congress prodded the Department of State, Defense, and the military that Stingers and the high levels of funding which, in the end, have proved vital, were provided. A National Security Council document, defining US policy as: seeking a Soviet withdrawal 'by all means available', was approved by the President in April 1985 and led to the aid flow increase. Arms aid went from $122 million in fiscal year 1984 to $280 million in fiscal year 1985, while the humanitarian aid programme was created from scratch, reaching, by fiscal year 1988, $30 million in cross-border USAID programmes and $10 million in direct humanitarian aid delivered to the Resistance in Pakistan and targeted for use inside Afghanistan. Since then, both US aid programmes have allowed the Afghans to sustain the increased anti-Soviet operations of 1985–6, which have led to the Soviets looking to a diplomatic rather than a military solution to the war.

There have been reports throughout the war of individual commanders selling weapons in the border bazaars. This is due, in part, to the fact that the Afghan Resistance has no central bureaucratic mechanism for turning in and re-issuing surplus equipment. It has also served as a way to convert both battlefield spoils and surplus aid weapons to cash; this was crucially important before the cross-border humanitarian aid and cash-for-food programmes became widespread. One result, however, is that there are now lots of ex-Resistance Kalashnikovs floating around Pakistan.

Stockpiling was also a reaction to the absence of a continued high-intensity conflict inside Afghanistan, especially early in the war. There was a widespread desire to have a supply of arms and ammunition available in case the Soviets pressed too hard or another dire need arose. Other resistance groups have pointed out Hezbi (Hekmatyar) as having a conscious policy of

Right: This is a bombed-out village near Herat, but it is a sight that can be seen throughout Afghanistan. It raises a vital issue: the critical importance of international support for relief and rehabilitation in Afghanistan if there is a Soviet withdrawal. The 1988 Geneva Accords contained no provision for any form of Soviet reparations or aid in rebuilding. The Resistance, for their part, have indicated that they would welcome such aid. (Massound Khalili, *Jamiat-e-Islami*)

stockpiling arms and ammunition for use after a Soviet withdrawal. Whether it was true or not cannot be confirmed, but it was certainly widely believed by other parties prior to 1985. Stockpiling has also resulted from instances where the supply of weapons runs ahead of the availability of men capable of using them. This seems, for example, to have been the motivating factor in Sayeff's party hoarding a number of SA-7s – which were betrayed to the Soviets in February 1984 – near Kabul. When the Geneva Accords were signed in 1988, the Resistance had amassed enough small-arms ammunition for a year of fighting. Other key elements, however, such as 107mm rockets, were only in sufficient supply for a few months' activity. Of the most critical single weapon, the Stinger, the Resistance had 'several hundred' according to one source and 350 according to another in May 1988.

Humanitarian aid, although the total amount expressed in dollars-per-Afghan getting into the country is low, is having a great impact on life inside Afghanistan in 1987–8. The availability of cheap grain in Pakistan has kept down prices throughout the border areas and has allowed grain from Kabul to be directed elsewhere, thus reducing the risk of famine. There have been claims that, of the humanitarian aid funnelled through the USAID programme which works with the Peshawar unity, only 15–20 per cent actually reaches Afghanistan (a figure hotly disputed by USAID) while 80–90 per cent of the aid channelled through private voluntary organizations reaches its destination. Tents, sleeping-bags, boots and blankets are still in short supply, but are making their way through Afghanistan. Even if much is sold off, the buyers are usually other Afghans.

6. THE FUTURE OF AFGHANISTAN

The Soviets have always stated that they want to leave Afghanistan. They have withdrawn from other countries that they have occupied in the past: Stalin pulled the Army out of Yugoslavia, Czechoslovakia, Norway, and North Korea in 1945 and North Iran in 1946; they withdrew from Austria and bases in Finland in the 1950s. The questions, in 1988, remain; are they going to withdraw from the whole of Afghanistan; do they still want to win the war despite any such withdrawal; if they do leave is it, in effect, an admission that the war is lost? It may be that they are not really looking for a face-saving way out of Afghanistan, but rather that they are giving the West a face-saving chance to withdraw support of the Resistance now, thus avoiding the need for a long-term Soviet approach that would rely on attrition and pressure against Pakistan to give them victory, cutting off the flow of aid that is key to the Resistance war effort.

From as early as 1980 the Soviets have always been willing to dangle the possibility of a withdrawal before the world. In 1985, Gorbachev apparently gave the militia a time-limit for battlefield success, which they did not meet within two years. The year 1988 was apparently Gorbachev's window of opportunity, either to settle in for the long haul or look for a diplomatic and political solution.

Will the Soviets complete their withdrawal from Afghanistan south of the Hindu Kush by early 1989? Despite rhetoric and apparent commitment to do so, it is not difficult to foresee a situation which would lead to a reduced commitment but a still active one, including aircraft and special operations forces as well as advisers remaining, especially in the north.

There are factors militating against such a long-term presence: the Soviet Press, by mid-1988, was looking at Afghanistan in a retrospective mode, and few Soviet soldiers will want to be among the last killed in an unpopular war. But to consider the military withdrawal from Afghanistan as being practically a *fait accompli* may be merely the latest in Western wishful thinking. The political and diplomatic efforts may still continue; the Soviets are certainly aware that while the Afghan Resistance may be formidable on the battlefield, it is weak politically and diplomatically. Nevertheless the guerrillas still control the vast majority of the countryside. The anti-Communist forces in Afghanistan in 1988 are not like those, for example, in eastern Europe after the Second World War. They are strong, cohesive, well armed and willing to fight for as long as they need to get their country back.

But in a guerrilla war, what happens on the battlefield does not always determine ultimate victory or defeat. The US in Vietnam, the Portuguese in Africa, the French in Algeria, and the Rhodesians were all winning militarily, but lost their wars. It remains to be seen whether Soviet military disengagement will mark the end of the war, or instead the start of a new and possibly more dangerous phase.

It is likely that, in conjunction with sympathetic nations, the Soviet, will attempt to increase diplomatic pressure against Pakistan, both bilaterally and in international organizations and forums. Certainly, if they were to halt their withdrawal short of completion, blaming Pakistan and the United States for the breakdown would be a necessity.

There is always the option of partition; dividing Afghanistan along the Hindu Kush and either making the north a dependent state (manned either by a rump Afghan

Communist government's forces or Soviet troops) or going farther and having the north hold a plebiscite and ask for admission as the sixteenth Republic of the Soviet Union. Rumours of this have been current among Afghan groups since early in the war. The apparent policy of 'regional differentiation' in parts of the north, shown by the emphasis on economic domination rather than de-population, suggest this may be a possible policy. Alternatively, the Soviets may withdraw to a phase line north of the Hindu Kush and no farther. A smaller security zone or rump state could be centred around Mazar-e-Sharif. In mid-1988, there were reports of increased efforts at consolidation in that area which would give an opportunity to pursue the option. Such a continued occupation, either direct or through surrogates, in the north could serve a purpose similar to Israel's security zone in south Lebanon.

In the Soviet Union, Afghanistan has become an unpopular war. Its monetary and prestige costs may prove an impediment to Gorbachev's consolidation of power and primary agenda of economic reform. The war is, most importantly, a barrier to better relations with the USA, Europe, China and the Third World. To the Soviets, Afghanistan has always been, and remains a peripheral issue. On the world stage, a truly major success would not be a subdued Afghanistan turned into a poorer version of Mongolia, but rather a reconciliation with China, a neutralized Europe and a globally impotent USA. If giving up their war in Afghanistan will help them attain this, it would be merely a tactical withdrawal.

Will the Resistance be able to take Kabul if the last Soviet troops leave it in February 1989? The most effective way would be not by direct assault, but by cutting the highways. This may be done if Massoud could concentrate the 13,000-man army he started forming in 1988 using his 800–1,400-man central forces as officers and apply them to this task. It is known that Massoud has been co-operating with commanders around Kabul for several years.

Unless they can hang on militarily, the PDPA will become a footnote in history. Najibullah, up to mid-1988, did not act as if he believed this, refusing to concentrate his outlying troops and continuing as if the war would go on as it always had. But this is likely to be merely show. There are also reports that at least one Najibullah speech at the PDPA Party Congress in November–December 1987, paying tribute to the Soviet role in Afghanistan, cast doubts on whether he believes that the PDPA regime can endure without Soviet armed forces. Backed by Soviet resources, the PDPA has had almost ten years to consolidate its power in Afghanistan and it has failed miserably. The divisions within the PDPA have increased since the accession of Najibullah. The new reality is much more complex than the *Parchim-Khalq* splits of the early 1980s. The *Parchim* now includes at least five identifiable factions while the *Khalqi* factions divide the Kabul-based leadership remaining from the 1980–6 period from those with differing military, geographical and tribal backgrounds. Warfare between PDPA factions is more likely in the wake of a Soviet withdrawal than warfare between Resistance parties. The PDPA could probably not survive the departure of Soviet troops except in a northern enclave, supported from Soviet territory. The fact that every senior PDPA official appears in public with Soviet rather than Afghan bodyguards underlines this fact. PDPA members – those that do not go to the Soviet Union – would not play any significant role in a post-war government. A coalition government including both the Resistance and the PDPA is simply not going to happen even if the Soviets sack Najibullah.

Once the Kabul regime military sees the Soviets have gone home, it will probably collapse, with whole units joining the Resistance. Afghans are realists; few are going to want to fight on grimly for a regime that would appear to be deserted by its only patron. Non-PDPA government workers will probably do the same.

The return of the King has been discussed throughout the war, first as a head of a Resistance, then as head of a government in exile, and finally as a possible participant in an interim government in Kabul. The King is both respected and divisive. He is respected because he was the last legitimate ruler of Afghanistan who could claim a broad consensus of legitimacy. He certainly was never

Above: Dud bombs remain a familiar sight in Afghanistan, but many of the children are now gone: deported to the Soviet Union for education (possibly more than 10,000), or as refugees to the cities, to

Pakistan or Iran. The Geneva Accords, signed in 1988, had no provision for the return of deportees from the Soviet Union. (Committee for a Free Afghanistan)

anti-Soviet throughout his reign. Many Afghans look upon the King's days with fondness, when it was summer all the year round: no bombs or helicopters or refugees. Others remember the corruption and the increasing Soviet influence. Islamist intellectuals are particularly resentful. Others remember that the King has, after all,

sat out the war in comfort in Italy. King Albert of the Belgians he most certainly is not.

There are fears that rivalries between the political leadership of the Peshawar-based parties, especially if Kabul were to fall, would lead to divisions in the Resistance, but Peshawar's influence will probably decline, rather than increase. It is the men with the Kalashnikovs in their hands who will control Afghanistan, much as it has been since the war began. It is likely that the authority of the parties over their commanders will decline as 1989 progresses, especially if the flow of arms aid is reduced. The commanders inside, however, are unlikely to abrogate their ties to their parties as long as some traditional ties of loyalty remain or they feel they can gain political leverage. The policy of Pakistan will also be vital in such a situation. If Pakistan decides to use parties or commanders as its 'chosen instrument' to influence events throughout the Pathan areas of Afghanistan, that will obviously be the key catalyst in the forming of any action against Kabul. Post-Zia, this is less likely.

Another possible splintering of the Resistance could come if a deal were made between the more revolutionary-oriented Resistance elements, especially Hekmatyar's Hezb, and elements of the regime, especially WAD. Other Afghans have seen the widespread reports of local Hekmatyar truces with Communist forces by late 1987 as indicating the depth and breadth of contacts with the regime. The Resistance could split if old-line élites, with pro-monarchist and moderate backgrounds, many of which worked together under Daoud's regime, come together on both sides. This would allow the PDPA to hand over to an on-paper non-Communist regime while the WAD and military remained intact, possibly all covered by a return of the King. India is believed to support this approach and the background of non-PDPA figures brought into government by mid-1988 suggest that this remains a possible Soviet objective. But the mere suggestion that the Soviets had their hand in such a deal would quite possibly be enough to kill it. Indian support is likely to be almost as fatal as Soviet support to any effort, considering that India is broadly hated throughout the Resistance. The deep divisions within the PDPA also make an organized deal less likely but as late as November 1988 it appeared to remain a Soviet goal.

A government in Kabul acceptable to Moscow – including the King or anyone else – could possibly survive only if it could get the support of some Resistance groups or leaders while others continued to fight against it. This sort of split in the Resistance has not occurred at any time in the war, which is unique for a Third World guerrilla war fought by so many conflicting elements. A situation with some groups backing a government in Kabul and others continuing to fight it would mean that the Soviets will have finally succeeded, despite a withdrawal, in getting other Afghans to fight Afghans, the traditional solution to problems in that part of the world. When combined with a security zone in the north, the Soviets might feel that an unstable Afghanistan poses no threat to their Islamic populations in Central Asia. As Aleksandr Prokhanov, one of the most prolific Soviet writers on the Afghan War, stated in the *Literaturnaya Gazeta* on 17 February 1988: 'Iran-style fundamentalism is no longer possible in the country . . . the threat of the emergence on the USSR's borders of an extremist Islamic regime prepared to take its propagandas and activities to our Central Asian republics – that threat will not be fulfilled'. Many observers of the Afghan Resistance would agree.

If the Soviets leave Afghanistan, it is unlikely that there will be a civil war or large-scale bloodshed. Certainly scores will be settled, and violence has long been a traditional Afghan means of resolving differences. The divisions between the Peshawar leadership may surface in fighting, but it is unlikely that the co-operation between the men who have been actually doing the fighting will vanish together with the Soviets. There has been relatively little – though by no means none – fighting between groups in the Resistance-controlled areas of Afghanistan in 1987–8 and it is unlikely that a Soviet withdrawal will work a dramatic change.

SOURCES

This is not a research volume – hence the absence of footnotes – but a briefing to suggest background, continuity and change in the war in Afghanistan.

Much of the information has been impressionistic or has come from a survey of the literature – which remains largely periodical – and from my trips with the *mujahideen* in 1984, 1985, 1987 and 1988. Extensive interviews have also provided much of the source material. I have asked many *mujahids* over the years – I have talked to many sources periodically since 1981 or before – to describe how they have seen the evolution of the war. For tracing the course of the fighting itself, most sources remain periodicals. The two most valuable were *Afghan Information Centre Monthly Bulletin* and *Afghan Realities*, mimeographed monthlies from Peshawar which collate news releases from both sides and interview people coming out of Afghanistan. On operations in the field since 1984, the monthly *Afghanistan Report* by the Institute of Strategic Studies, Islamabad, is valuable. But the daily reports that have been in the Press in New York and Washington, London, Paris and Pakistan cover most of the day-to-day happenings. These were supplemented by the translations of foreign broadcasts and new reports translated by the BBC and the US FBIS.

Books used as sources on the war itself include: Henry Bradsher's *Afghanistan and the Soviet Union*, 2nd edition, 1985, Chapel Hill, N.C., probably the most thorough account to date. Anthony Arnold's *Afghanistan: The Soviet Invasion in Perspective*, 2nd edition, Stanford, 1985, concentrates on the invasion and the events leading up to it – another excellent work. The same author's *Afghanistan's Two Party Communism*, Stanford, 1983, details the internal political situation and its background. The second editions of the Bradsher and Arnold books were the source for much of the pre-1986 information on political consolidation.

Joseph Collins's *The Soviet Invasion of Afghanistan. A Study in the Use of Force in Soviet Foreign Policy*, Lexington, Massachussets, 1986 looks at the invasion from the Soviet strategic angle, but includes much of value on the first years of the war as well. Edward Giradet's *Afghanistan: The Soviet War*, New York, 1985, draws heavily on the author's extensive experience inside Afghanistan with the Resistance. David C. Isby's *Russia's War in Afghanistan*, London, 1985, is a slim volume, but the source of much information. Mark Urban's *War in Afghanistan*, London, 1987, focusses on the military situation from the Communist side. Thomas Hammond's *Red Flag Over Afghanistan*, Boulder, 1984, is a critical and well-reasoned study.

On the Resistance, the best book by far is Olivier Roy's *Islam and the Afghan Resistance*, Cambridge, 1986. Louis Dupree's *Afghanistan*, Princeton, 1981, is the best single background book on people and country. The US Government Printing Office's *Area Handbook: Afghanistan* (latest edition, 1987) is also worthwhile. J. Bruce Amstutz, *Afghanistan. The First Five Years of Soviet Occupation*, Washington, D.C., 1986, is large and comprehensive if something of a grab-bag. In French, Michael Barry's 1984 *Le Royaume d'Insolence* is outstanding for its treatment of the Afghans and the Resistance. Brief, informative but dated volumes are Gerard Challiand's *Report From Afghanistan*, New York, 1981 and John Fullerton's *The Soviet Occupation of Afghanistan*, Hong Kong, 1983. Two excellent works on the human rights situation are Barnett Rubin's *Tears, Blood and Cries*, New Haven, 1984, and *To Die in Afghanistan*, New Haven, 1985. On the details of Soviet hardware and tactics is David C. Isby's *Weapons and Tactics of the Soviet Army*, revised edition, London, 1988.

Valuable books of essays include Ralph Magnus, ed. *Afghan Alternatives*, New Brunswick, NJ, 1985; Grant M. Farr and John G. Merriam, eds., *Afghan Resistance, the Politics of Survival*, Boulder, 1987; and Rosanne Klass, ed. *Afghanistan, the Great Game Revisited*, New York, 1988.

Annual sources include mentions in a number of volumes, such as the International Institute of Strategic Studies' *Strategic Survey* and the US annual human rights report. The annual *Afghanistan* volume edited by Dr. A. Stahel from the

Swiss Library for the Study of Afghanistan has excellent military analysis. Craig Karp's *Afghanistan: Seven Years of Soviet Occupation*. U.S. Department of State Special Report, No. 155, December 1986 is in a series of reports dating to 1980. The comparing and contrasting of the annual State Department reports was one of the ways to delineate the changing Soviet approaches to Afghanistan.

The sources on battlefield operations and tactics are surprisingly limited and are an area where good, well-documented work is needed. This has led to much reliance on periodicals. The various publications of the French *Bureau International Afghan* (B.I.A.) are outstanding, but a few of the most notable English-language articles include: John Gunston's 'SU-24s, TU-16s Support Soviet Armed Forces', *Aviation Week and Space Technology*, 29 October 1984, pp. 40–3. Joseph Collins's 'The Soviet Military Experience in Afghanistan', *Military Review*, May 1985, pp. 16–28. David C. Isby's, 'Soviet Tactics in the War in Afghanistan', *Jane's Defence Review*, vol. 4, no. 7, 1983, pp. 681–93. Douglas Hart's, 'Low Intensity Conflict in Afghanistan, The Soviet

View', *Survival*, March–April 1982, pp. 61–7. Jiri Valenta's, 'From Prague to Kabul: The Soviet Style of Invasion', *International Security*, Fall, 1980, pp. 124–7. Colonel Ali Ahmad Jalali, 'The Soviet Military Operation in Afghanistan and the Role of Light and Heavy Forces at Tactical and Operational Level', *Report of Proceedings, Boeing Light Infantry Conference, 1985*, (Seattle) pp. 161–81. (This is a really useful source and the excellent maps of the Kunar and Khost operations are the source of much of what the author knows on these actions). David Isby's 'Soviet Special Operations Forces in Afghanistan, 1979–85', *Report of Proceedings, Boeing Light Infantry Conference 1985*, (Seattle) pp. 182–97. The Russian-language articles became much more useful under *glasnost* in 1987–8.

Useful first person accounts include: Jan Goodwin, *Caught in the Crossfire*, New York, 1986. Jere Van Dyk, *In Afghanistan*, New York, 1983. Sandy Gall, *Behind Russian Lines*, London, 1983. Nigel Ryan, *A Hitch or Two in Afghanistan*, London, 1983. Mike Martin, *Afghanistan: Inside a Rebel Stronghold*, Poole, Dorset, 1984. Peregrine Hodson, *Under a Sickle Moon*, New York, 1987.

Below: Moving past a concealed Resistance position, this Soviet BMD airborne infantry fighting vehicle was part of the 'point' detachment of a convoy. The Soviets would put such detachments ahead of all their major convoys and troop columns, often heavily reinforced with engineer elements to repair the road, remove obstacles and detect and lift mines. (Committee for a Free Afghanistan, Ben Pendleton)

INDEX